THE PRESIDENTS

VISUAL ENCYCLOPEDIA

DK Delhi

Project Editor Suefa Lee
Project Art Editor Divya PR
Assistant Editor Riji Raju
Art Editor Anjali Sachar
Assistant Art Editors Yashashvi Choudhary, Simar Dhamija
DTP Designers Sachin Gupta, Ashok Kumar
Senior DTP Designer Harish Aggarwal
Picture Researcher Sakshi Saluja
Jacket Designers Surabhi Wadhwa
Managing Jackets Editor Saloni Singh
Pre-production Manager Balwant Singh
Production Manager Pankaj Sharma
Picture Research Manager Taiyaba Khatoon
Senior Managing Editor Rohan Sinha
Deputy Managing Art Editor Anjana Nair

DK London

Assistant Editor Vicky Richards
Senior Art Editor Spencer Holbrook
Senior Editor Fleur Star
US Senior Editor Margaret Parrish
US Editor Jill Hamilton
Jacket Editor Claire Gell
Jacket Design Development Manager Sophia MTT
Producer, Pre-production Nadine King
Producer Gary Batchelor
Managing Editor Francesca Baines
Managing Art Editor Philip Letsu
Publisher Andrew Macintyre
Associate Publishing Director Liz Wheeler
Art Director Karen Self
Publishing Director Jonathan Metcalf

Written by Philip Parker
Consultant: Gary Werner

First American Edition, 2017
Published in the United States by DK Publishing
345 Hudson Street, New York, New York 10014

Published in Great Britain by Dorling Kindersley Limited.

A catalog record for this book is available from the Library of
Congress.

ISBN 978-1-4654-5853-7

DK books are available at special discounts when purchased in
bulk for sales promotions, premiums, fund-raising, or educational
use. For details, contact: DK Publishing Special Markets, 345 Hudson
Street, New York, New York 10014 or SpecialSales@dk.com
Printed in USA

A WORLD OF IDEAS:
SEE ALL THERE IS TO KNOW

www.dk.com

SMITHSONIAN

THE PRESIDENTS

VISUAL ENCYCLOPEDIA

CONTENTS

1

2

NOTABLE FIRST LADIES   124

3

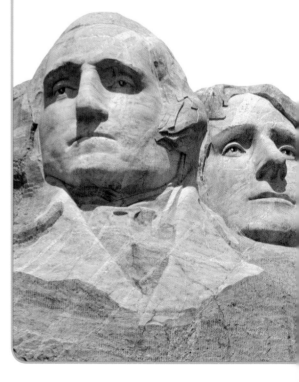

4

THE CONSTITUTION AND THE PRESIDENCY   146

PRESIDENTIAL PLACES AND VEHICLES   172

5

COLOR KEY

This book uses different colors to show the political party of each president.

★ Republican

★ Democrat

★ Other parties or independents

1 PRESIDENTS

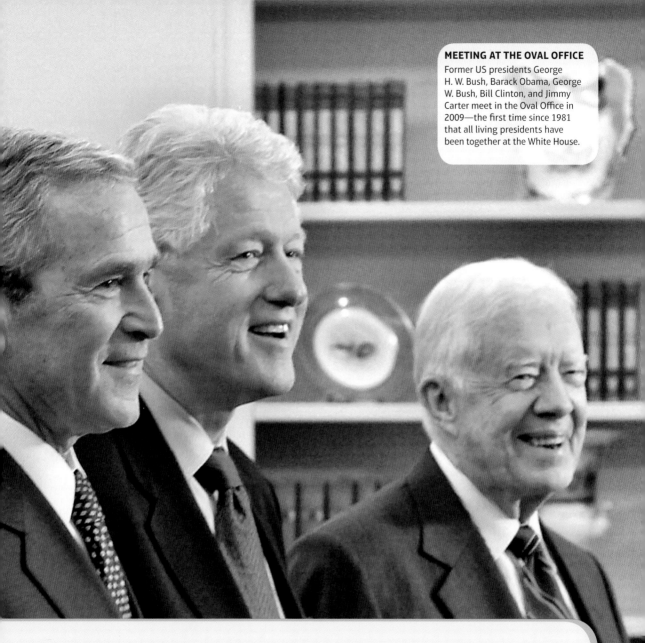

Since George Washington took the first oath in 1789, 44 people have held the presidential office. As the nation's chief executive, presidents throughout the years have faced many domestic and international challenges in ensuring the prosperity and security of the United States.

GEORGE WASHINGTON

1st ★ 1789–1797

George Washington was a military officer who became famous for leading the Continental Army to victory against the British. Known as the "Father of the Country," he played a vital role in drafting the US Constitution. His refusal to take sides in political disputes made him an obvious choice for the first president, and he remains the only president to have been elected unanimously. A unifying figure, Washington also forged several treaties with Britain and France to avoid US involvement in foreign wars.

CROSSING THE DELAWARE

This painting gives an artist's view of Washington leading his soldiers across the icy Delaware River on Christmas Day, 1776. (In reality, he would never have been so dangerously perched at the front of the boat.) The attack took the British by surprise, and they were defeated at the Battle of Trenton.

DATA FILE

BORN: February 22, 1732, Westmoreland County, Virginia
DIED: December 14, 1799

INAUGURATED AS PRESIDENT: April 30, 1789, age 57

KEY DATES:

1775 Becomes commander of the Continental Army.

1781 Defeats the British at Yorktown, ending the American Revolution.

1787 Is the first person to sign the United States Constitution.

1793 Begins his second term as president. The Constitution does not specify whether a president can do so, so his actions set a precedent.

1797 Retires to his plantation in Virginia.

☞ Martha Washington pp126–27

☞ The American Revolution p148

☞ The Drafting of the Constitution pp150–51

Washington's second **inaugural address** is the **shortest** given by any president— just **135 words**.

George Washington

REVIEWING THE TROOPS

George Washington reviews the troops gathered at Fort Cumberland, Maryland, on October 18, 1794, before their march to put down the Whiskey Rebellion.

WHISKEY REBELLION

In 1791, to help pay off a large national debt, Washington introduced a new federal tax on distilled spirits, including whiskey. Farmers in Pennsylvania protested and hundreds of armed rebels attacked federal officers. In August 1794, Washington sent an army of 15,000 militiamen to enforce this tax. As the army marched into Pennsylvania, the rebels melted away. The tax was abolished in 1801.

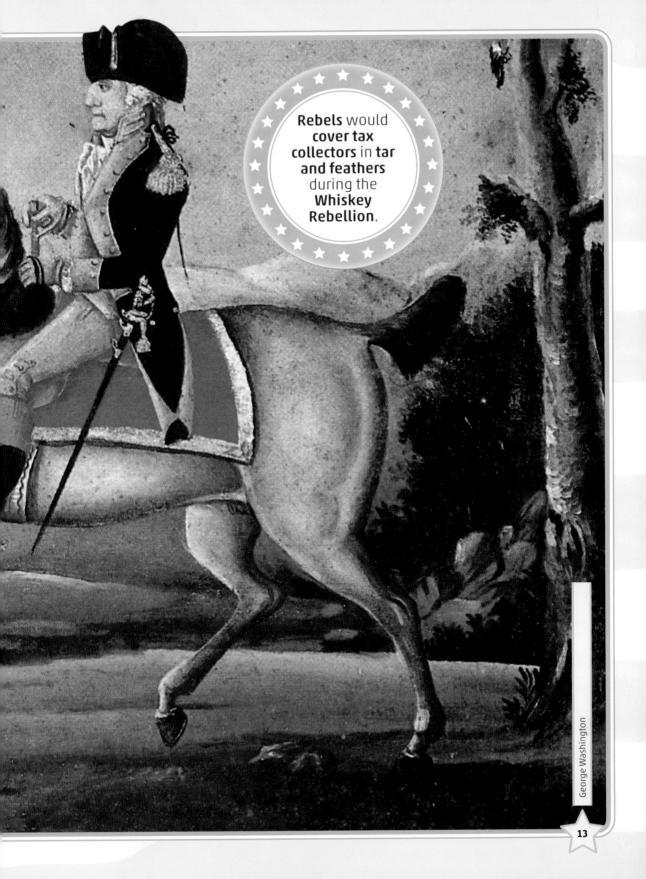

Rebels would **cover tax collectors** in **tar and feathers** during the **Whiskey Rebellion**.

George Washington

JOHN ADAMS

2nd ★ 1797–1801

Federalist

A lawyer by profession, John Adams served as an important diplomat in Europe, where he negotiated the treaty that ended the American Revolution. During his presidency, when the threat of a war with France loomed large, Adams established a naval force and was honored as the "Father of the Navy." However, he became unpopular after the Alien and Sedition Acts were passed. These were laws that made it an offense to criticize government officials and allowed non-Americans (aliens) to be deported more easily.

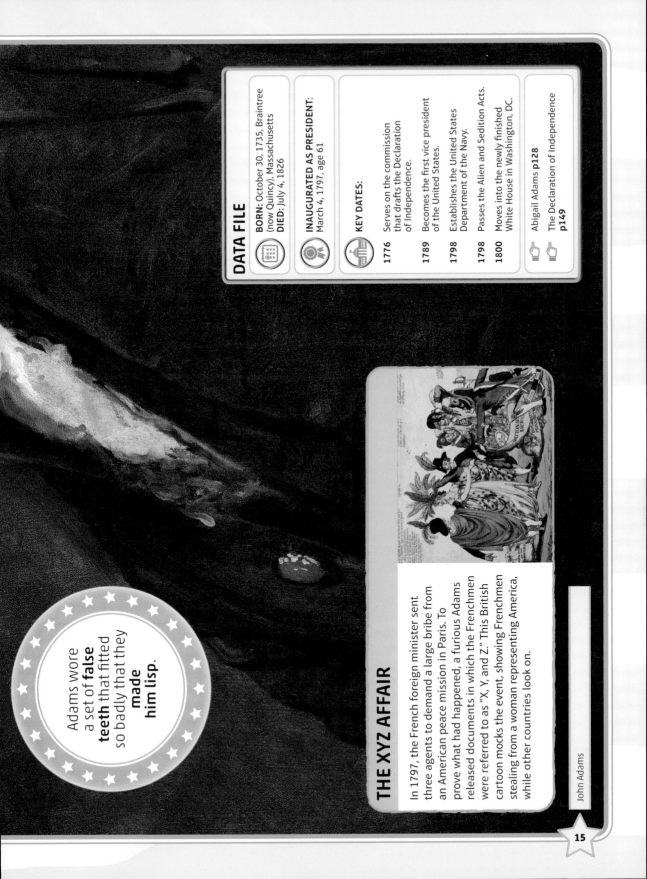

DATA FILE

BORN: October 30, 1735, Braintree (now Quincy), Massachusetts
DIED: July 4, 1826

INAUGURATED AS PRESIDENT: March 4, 1797, age 61

KEY DATES:

1776 Serves on the commission that drafts the Declaration of Independence.

1789 Becomes the first vice president of the United States.

1798 Establishes the United States Department of the Navy.

1798 Passes the Alien and Sedition Acts.

1800 Moves into the newly finished White House in Washington, DC.

Abigail Adams **p128**

The Declaration of Independence **p149**

Adams wore a set of **false teeth** that fitted so badly that they **made him lisp.**

THE XYZ AFFAIR

In 1797, the French foreign minister sent three agents to demand a large bribe from an American peace mission in Paris. To prove what had happened, a furious Adams released documents in which the Frenchmen were referred to as "X, Y, and Z." This British cartoon mocks the event, showing Frenchmen stealing from a woman representing America, while other countries look on.

John Adams

THOMAS JEFFERSON

3rd ★ 1801–1809   *Democratic-Republican*

A gifted scholar and lawyer, Thomas Jefferson was the main author of the Declaration of Independence and the first US Secretary of State. As president, he reduced the national debt, but made himself unpopular by forbidding foreign trade to avoid becoming involved in the war between France and Britain.

DATA FILE

BORN: April 13, 1743, Goochland (now Albemarle) County, Virginia
DIED: July 4, 1826

INAUGURATED AS PRESIDENT: March 4, 1801, age 57

KEY DATES:

1776 Drafts the Declaration of Independence.

1801 Becomes the first president to be inaugurated in Washington, DC, the new federal capital.

1807 Signs the Embargo Act forbidding trade with foreign powers. It is unpopular with businesses and farmers, and is repealed in 1809.

1819 Establishes the University of Virginia.

☞ The Declaration of Independence **p149**

Jefferson's **6,500-volume library** became the core collection of the **Library of Congress**.

SALUTING THE FLAG

Soldiers in New Orleans fire a salute as the American flag is raised and the French flag lowered after the Louisiana Purchase.

THE LOUISIANA PURCHASE

In 1803, Jefferson seized the opportunity to acquire Louisiana from the French Emperor Napoleon for $15 million. It was a vast area of 828,000 sq miles (2,144,510 sq km), which stretched from New Orleans to Montana. This doubled the size of the United States and opened up the territories to the west.

Thomas Jefferson

A HELPING HAND

During their two-year-long journey, Lewis and Clark came across many Native American groups. Sacagawea, a Shoshone woman whom they met in Dakota, became their interpreter and helped them establish peaceful relations with the Native Americans they met.

THE LEWIS AND CLARK EXPEDITION

After the Louisiana Purchase, Jefferson decided to send an expedition to explore the new territory. It was led by Meriwether Lewis, Jefferson's private secretary, and William Clark, a former army officer. The Corps of Discovery, as the expedition became known, set out from Missouri in May 1804. They did not find a river route from the US to the Pacific Ocean, as Jefferson had hoped for, but managed to cross the Rocky Mountains and reach the ocean nonetheless. During this journey, the group kept a detailed account of the plants and animals they saw, and made extensive maps of the lands they crossed.

Thomas Jefferson

JAMES MADISON

4th ★ 1809-1817   *Democratic-Republican*

James Madison was popularly known as the "Father of the Constitution." He believed the government should have only the powers granted to it by the Constitution. Madison played a key role in introducing the Bill of Rights, which amended the Constitution and further secured the rights of citizens. His presidency was dominated by growing tensions with Britain and the war that then ensued.

DATA FILE

BORN: March 16, 1751, Port Conway, Virginia
DIED: June 28, 1836

INAUGURATED AS PRESIDENT: March 4, 1809, age 57

KEY DATES:

1787 Begins writing the Federalist Papers, a series of essays that urged New York voters to ratify the Constitution.

1812 **JUNE 18** Issues a declaration of war against Britain.

☞ Dolley Madison **p129**

☞ The Drafting of the Constitution **pp150–51**

☞ The Bill of Rights **pp158–59**

The extremely rare **$5,000 bill** features a **portrait of Madison**.

THE WAR OF 1812

In 1812, a powerful group of young politicians, called the "War Hawks," strongly urged Madison to declare war on Britain. They wanted to stop British ships from harrassing American vessels and to take land in Canada, which was still a British colony. Reluctantly, Madison gave in and a military conflict ensued. Although the Americans were initially able to repel British ships, they made little progress advancing into Canada. In 1814, British troops occupied Washington and burned the White House. Later that year, the two sides signed a peace treaty at Ghent, in Belgium, to end the war.

BATTLE OF NEW ORLEANS
Andrew Jackson (on horseback) is shown leading the defense of New Orleans against the British in January 1815. Although the Americans won this battle, it took place two weeks after a peace treaty had been signed, as news traveled slowly at the time.

James Madison

JAMES MONROE

5th ★ 1817–1825 *Democratic-Republican*

James Monroe's extensive political experience as governor of Virginia prepared him well for the presidency. During his first term, he expanded the country with the acquisition of Florida from Spain. He also had to deal with the issue of slavery, which was permitted in the southern states but had been abolished in the north. When Missouri wanted to join the Union as a slave state, Monroe signed a compromise bill, which stated that the number of slave-holding and free states should be equal. During his second term, Monroe issued a bold policy called the "Monroe Doctrine," in which the United States declared its opposition to any European interference in North and South America.

Monroe **died on July 4**—the **third president** to have died **on that date**.

MANY YEARS OF SERVICE

By the time Monroe's presidency drew to an end, he had served the United States for 50 years—holding more government offices than any president before or after him. He is pictured here as a young man, but Monroe was 58 years old when he became president.

DATA FILE

BORN: April 28, 1758, Westmoreland County, Virginia
DIED: July 4, 1831

INAUGURATED AS PRESIDENT: March 4, 1817, age 58

KEY DATES:

1799 Serves as governor of Virginia.

1811 Appointed as Secretary of State.

1814 Serves as Secretary of War.

1819 Purchases Florida from Spain for $5 million. This becomes a territory of the US, with its own government, but is not admitted as a state until 1845.

1820 Signs the Missouri Compromise, which admits Missouri to the Union as a slave state, but also admits Maine as a free state.

1823 Announces the Monroe Doctrine in his annual message to Congress.

James Monroe

JOHN QUINCY ADAMS

6th ★ 1825–1829   *Democratic-Republican*

The son of former president John Adams, John Quincy Adams was the first president whose father had also held the same office. In his early career, he was a successful diplomat and served as an ambassador to several European countries before becoming Secretary of State. In this position, he played a key role in negotiating the Adams-Onis Treaty with Spain, which gave the United States control over Florida. After becoming president, Adams proposed the building of new roads and canals. However, he had weak political backing and his plans gained little support.

> " If your **actions inspire** others to **dream** more, **learn** more, **do** more, and **become** more, you are a **leader**. "

DEATH IN THE HOUSE

After losing the 1828 presidential election, Adams returned to politics as a representative for Massachusetts. He became the only former president to enter Congress. In 1848, while seated in the House Chamber, Adams suffered a stroke, and died two days later.

DATA FILE

BORN: July 11, 1767, Braintree (now Quincy), Massachusetts
DIED: February 23, 1848

INAUGURATED AS PRESIDENT: March 4, 1825, age 57

KEY DATES:

1819   Negotiates the Adams-Onis Treaty with Spain.

1825   Chosen to be president by the House of Representatives because no candidate had gained a clear majority of the Electoral College votes.

1828   **MAY 19** Signs a bill that increases the tax paid by importers. It becomes known as the "Tariff of Abominations."

ANDREW JACKSON

7th ★ 1829–1837   *Democrat*

An iconic war hero, Andrew Jackson was the first president to be elected for the newly formed Democratic party. His politics, called "Jacksonian Democracy," aimed to defend the rights of ordinary American citizens. Nicknamed "Old Hickory" for his toughness, Jackson threatened to send troops to South Carolina when the state refused to impose a high tariff (tax on imported goods). He also ordered the enforcement of the Indian Removal Act, which displaced many Native American groups from their homelands. In 1835, he became the first president to suffer an assassination attempt, but escaped unharmed by beating his attacker off with his walking cane.

PRESIDENTIAL INAUGURATION

Jackson was inaugurated as president on the East Portico of the United States Capitol building. The White House was opened for a reception afterward, but the crowd grew so large and rowdy that they destroyed furniture and china, and Jackson himself had to be led away for his safety.

DATA FILE

BORN: March 15, 1767, Waxhaw, South Carolina
DIED: June 8, 1845

INAUGURATED AS PRESIDENT: March 4, 1829, age 61

KEY DATES:

1815 Leads his troops to victory against the British Army in the Battle of New Orleans.

1830 Signs the Indian Removal Act.

1832 Asks Congress for authority to send troops to South Carolina, which had refused to impose a high tariff on imported goods.

1832 Vetoes a bill to set up the Second Bank of the United States, claiming that the bank is unconstitutional.

After being **shot** in a **duel,** Jackson had a **bullet lodged** in his **chest** for **40 years**.

Andrew Jackson

MARTIN VAN BUREN

8th ★ 1837–1841   *Democrat*

Born into a struggling family of Dutch descent, Martin Van Buren could not afford to go to college but studied law independently before entering politics. He spent much of his presidency dealing with a severe economic recession, although his budget cuts made this worse. Van Buren also opposed the extension of slavery to new states, blocking Texas from joining the Union as a slave state.

DATA FILE

BORN: December 5, 1782, Kinderhook, New York
DIED: July 24, 1862

INAUGURATED AS PRESIDENT: March 4, 1837, age 54

KEY DATES:

1837 Calls for a special session of Congress in response to the Panic of 1837, which had caused an economic depression.

1839 Prevents war between militias in Maine and the Canadian province of New Brunswick over a border dispute.

1840 Signs the Independent Treasury Act, which separates government funds from private banks. Van Buren proposed this act due to the recession earlier in his term, which was caused by the banks.

The word "okay" originates from Van Buren's nickname "Old Kinderhook."

THE TRAIL OF TEARS

The Indian Removal Act of 1830 gave the president the right to relocate Native Americans to west of the Mississippi River in exchange for their lands in the southeast. Seminoles, Creeks, and Chickasaws were removed against their will, but the Cherokees fought against their removal in court. However, in 1836, a treaty was forced upon them and they were given two years to leave their lands. In November 1838, Van Buren sent federal troops to force them westward. Around 5,000 died during this harrowing journey, falling victim to harsh weather, disease, and lack of food.

Martin Van Buren

WILLIAM HENRY
HARRISON

9th ★ March–April 1841   *Whig*

A celebrated war hero, William Henry Harrison won the nickname "Old Tip" after he defeated the Native American Chief Tecumseh at the Battle of Tippecanoe Creek. Having had a successful career in the army, he entered politics, and went on to became the governor of the Indiana Territory. Harrison later stood for two presidential elections, winning in 1840 and becoming the first president from the Whig party. However, he gave his inaugural address on a cold March morning without a coat or hat, leading to a fatal bout of pneumonia. Harrison died a month later, becoming the shortest-serving president in the history of the United States.

Harrison's **inaugural address** was the **longest** ever, at one hour and 45 minutes.

DATA FILE

📅 **BORN:** February 9, 1773, Berkeley, Virginia
DIED: April 4, 1841

🎖️ **INAUGURATED AS PRESIDENT:** March 4, 1841, age 68

🏛️ **KEY DATES:**

1791 Joins the army as a junior commissioned officer.

1798 Begins his early political career, becoming secretary of the Northwest Territory.

1800 Becomes governor of the Indiana Territory.

1811 Defeats the Shawnee chief Tecumseh at the Battle of Tippecanoe Creek.

1840 Wins the presidential election with 230 Electoral College votes to Martin Van Buren's 70.

👉 Political Parties **pp200–01**

WHIG PROPAGANDA

During the election of 1840, Harrison's Whig party portrayed him as a simple man, brought up in a log cabin. They made posters such as this one, showing him greeting fellow war veterans, in order to contrast him with his luxury-loving opponent. The propaganda worked, and Harrison won easily.

William Henry Harrison

JOHN TYLER

10th ★ 1841–1845

Whig

Originally elected as vice president, John Tyler became the first president to take office because of the death of his predecessor. Although like Harrison he was a member of the Whig party, he did not share many of its views. He supported states' rights, including their right to protect slavery. During his time in office, he vetoed a bill to set up a national bank, although his party supported it. As a result, he became unpopular with the Whigs, and was not chosen as their candidate in the 1844 election.

Tyler was the father of **15 children**—the **most** of any president.

THE ANNEXATION OF TEXAS

After a lengthy military conflict, Texas declared itself independent from Mexico in 1836. Because it had a large number of American settlers, many Texans wanted to join the United States and Tyler supported them, annexing the state in 1845. Here, the Texas flag flies over the Alamo (a famous battle site) in celebration.

DATA FILE

BORN: March 29, 1790, Charles City County, Virginia
DIED: January 18, 1862

INAUGURATED AS PRESIDENT:
April 6, 1841, age 51

KEY DATES:

1841 Vetoes a bill to set up a national bank. This leads to his entire Cabinet resigning.

1844 Marries Julia Gardiner and becomes the first president to get married while in office.

1845 Signs bills admitting Florida and Texas into the Union as the 27th and 28th states.

John Tyler

JAMES K. POLK

11th ★ 1845–1849   Democrat

Previously the governor of Tennessee, James K. Polk was relatively unknown when he ran for office. He believed in the theory of "Manifest Destiny," the idea that the United States was destined to expand across North America, and he promised to complete the annexation of Texas, settle the dispute with Britain over the boundaries of Oregon, and acquire land in California. As president, Polk achieved all these aims, and captained a great territorial expansion of the United States. He decided not to run for a second term, and stepped down in 1849.

DATA FILE

BORN: November 2, 1795, Mecklenburg County, North Carolina
DIED: June 15, 1849

INAUGURATED AS PRESIDENT: March 4, 1845, age 49

KEY DATES:

1825   Elected to the House of Representatives.

1846   **MAY 13** Signs a declaration of war against Mexico.

1846   Signs a bill reducing import tariffs to low levels and another establishing local subtreasuries to manage federal funds.

> No president who **performs his duties faithfully** and **conscientiously** can have any **leisure**.

Presidents

34

THE MEXICAN WAR

Although Texas had been annexed, there continued to be disagreement between the United States and Mexico over the southern border of Texas. In 1846, Polk sent General Zachary Taylor and his troops to the disputed area. When the Mexicans attacked the American forces, war was declared. General Taylor won several victories against the Mexicans, even capturing additional land in Mexico. In 1848, the Treaty of Guadalupe Hidalgo was signed, which made the river, Rio Grande, the boundary between Texas and Mexico and gave the United States additional land in California and New Mexico.

BATTLE OF RESACA DE LA PALMA
United States cavalry units are shown charging the Mexican army at the Battle of Resaca de la Palma on May 9, 1846. General Zachary Taylor's victory forced the Mexican troops to retreat south of the Rio Grande river.

James K. Polk

ZACHARY TAYLOR

12th ★ 1849–1850

Whig

A career army officer, Zachary Taylor's success as one of the commanders in the Mexican War of 1846 made him a war hero. Nicknamed "Old Rough and Ready" for his willingness to get things done, he was highly popular and won the 1848 election despite his lack of political experience. Although he was a slave owner himself, Taylor discouraged the extension of slavery to new territories and states. He tried to hold the Union together by opposing the Compromise of 1850, which would permit federal territories in the west (areas owned by the United States but not officially recognized as states), such as Utah, to allow slavery.

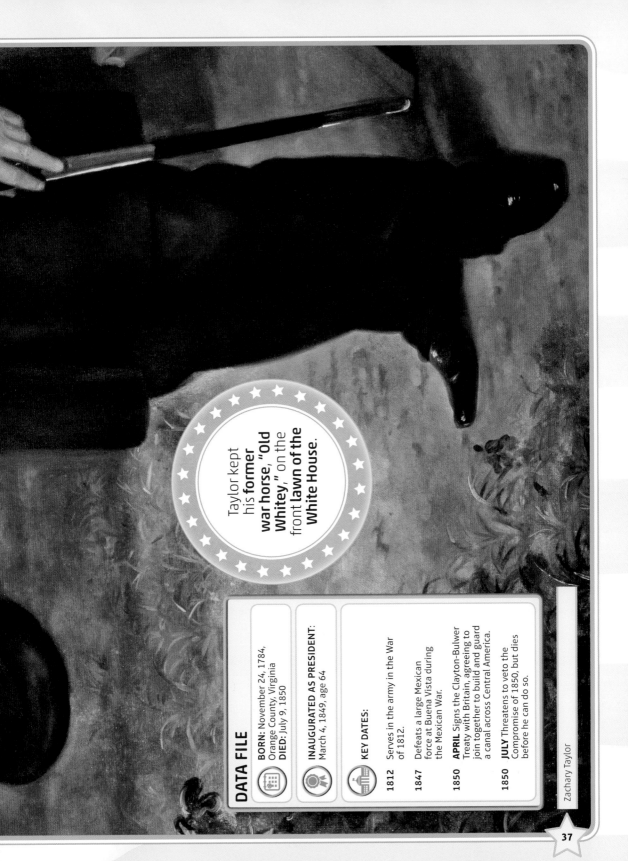

Taylor kept his **former war horse, "Old Whitey,"** on the **front lawn of the White House.**

DATA FILE

BORN: November 24, 1784, Orange County, Virginia
DIED: July 9, 1850

INAUGURATED AS PRESIDENT: March 4, 1849, age 64

KEY DATES:

1812 Serves in the army in the War of 1812.

1847 Defeats a large Mexican force at Buena Vista during the Mexican War.

1850 **APRIL** Signs the Clayton-Bulwer Treaty with Britain, agreeing to join together to build and guard a canal across Central America.

1850 **JULY** Threatens to veto the Compromise of 1850, but dies before he can do so.

Zachary Taylor

MILLARD FILLMORE

13th ★ 1850–1853   *Whig*

Born to a poor farming family, Millard Fillmore was a self-taught lawyer whose presidency began unexpectedly when President Taylor died. The issue of slavery dominated his time in office, but he took a different approach from his predecessor by supporting the Compromise of 1850. This allowed California to become a free state, but also permitted slavery in Utah and New Mexico. It also included controversial measures for dealing with runaway slaves. His actions outraged the northerners and widened the gap between the free and slave states.

Fillmore began **formal school** at the **age of 19**, and ended up **marrying** his **teacher**.

DATA FILE

BORN: January 7, 1800, Cayuga County, New York
DIED: March 8, 1874

INAUGURATED AS PRESIDENT: July 10, 1850, age 50

KEY DATES:

1832   Elected to the House of Representatives.

1850   **AUGUST** Sends 750 federal troops to stop the state of Texas from invading New Mexico over a border issue.

1850   **SEPTEMBER** Signs the Compromise of 1850, including the Fugitive Slave Act, which made the federal government responsible for catching and returning runaway slaves.

PERRY'S MISSION TO JAPAN

Fillmore wanted to establish a trade link with Japan, which had refused to trade with foreign powers for over 200 years. In 1853, he sent Commodore Matthew Perry with a fleet of four ships to visit Japan. The mission led to the opening of Japanese ports to American ships and four years later, a trade agreement between the two countries was signed.

Millard Fillmore

FRANKLIN PIERCE

14th ★ 1853–1857   *Democrat*

Having previously served as both a representative and senator, Franklin Pierce was elected president in 1852 when the Democrats could not agree between four other contenders. His presidency was overshadowed by the debate over whether to allow slavery in Kansas. A supporter of westward expansion, he promoted the Gadsden Purchase by which the United States acquired land in northern Mexico. He also threatened war against Spain if it did not sell Cuba.

DATA FILE

BORN: November 23, 1804, Hillsboro, New Hampshire
DIED: October 8, 1869

INAUGURATED AS PRESIDENT: March 4, 1853, age 48

KEY DATES:

1847   Serves in the army during the Mexican War.

1854   **APRIL** Signs the treaty authorizing the Gadsden Purchase, which acquires land from Mexico for $10 million.

1854   Issues the Ostend Manifesto, which threatens to take Cuba from Spain by force.

Pierce gave his **3,319-word inaugural** address from **memory**—with **no notes**.

THE KANSAS-NEBRASKA ACT

In 1854, Pierce signed the Kansas-Nebraska Act, allowing each of the two territories to decide if they wanted to enter the Union as slave states (states where slavery was permitted). The Act opposed the Missouri Compromise of 1820, which banned slavery in the region. It reignited the disagreement between the proslavery and antislavery forces in Kansas, and led to a period of political chaos and bloodshed.

BORDER RUFFIANS

Thousands of proslavery settlers, called "Border Ruffians," streamed into Kansas after the Kansas-Nebraska Act. They wanted to make sure that Kansas became a slave state and clashed violently with "Free Staters," who opposed this.

Franklin Pierce

JAMES **BUCHANAN**

15th ★ 1857-1861

Democrat

Known as "Old Buck," James Buchanan was 65 when he was elected and had a wealth of political experience behind him. However, like his predecessors, much of his presidency was spent dealing with growing tensions over the issue of slavery. He supported the Dred Scott decision by the Supreme Court, which ruled that slaves were not citizens, and was also in favor of allowing Kansas to be admitted as a slave state. This made him popular in the south, but growing abolitionist demands in the north led southern politicians to believe no compromise was possible. By the end of his term, seven southern states had left the Union.

Buchanan is the **only president** to have **never** been **married**.

JOHN BROWN'S RAID

On October 16, 1859, a group of abolitionists led by John Brown attacked the federal armory at Harpers Ferry, Virginia. The group wanted to use the weapons stored there to start a slave revolt. However, Buchanan sent US marines to fight the raiders, and Brown's plan failed. Although his actions were praised by some northerners, he was found guilty of treason and hanged.

DATA FILE

BORN: April 23, 1791, Cove Gap, Pennsylvania
DIED: June 1, 1868

INAUGURATED AS PRESIDENT:
March 4, 1857, age 65

KEY DATES:

1820 Elected to the House of Representatives.

1857 Promotes the Lecompton Constitution, which supported admitting Kansas to the Union as a slave state.

1866 Publishes the first presidential memoir, *Mr. Buchanan's Administration on the Eve of the Rebellion.*

James Buchanan

ABRAHAM LINCOLN

16th ★ 1861-1865 *Republican*

President Abraham Lincoln's strong leadership saved the United States from a permanent split. Born into a poor Kentucky family, he taught himself law and became a prominent opponent of slavery. The first Republican president, his victory in the presidential election sparked the breakaway of the southern, proslavery states, which came together to form the Confederate States of America. They attacked the Union (the loyal US states) at Fort Sumter, South Carolina, in 1861. In the Civil War that ensued, Lincoln guided the north (Unionists) through a period of military defeat until its advantage in industry and manpower finally secured its victory. Tragically, Lincoln was assassinated shortly after the end of the war.

GETTYSBURG ADDRESS
In July 1863, the north won a major victory against the south at Gettysburg, Pennsylvania, losing 40,000 men in the battle. During the dedication of a new cemetery there, Lincoln delivered one of the most famous speeches in American history.

Presidents

> We here **highly resolve** that these **dead** shall **not** have **died in vain**, that this **nation under God** shall have a **new birth of freedom**, and that **government of the people, by the people, for the people** shall **not perish** from the **earth.**
>
> Abraham Lincoln, Gettysburg Address

DATA FILE

BORN: February 12, 1809, Hodgenville, Kentucky
DIED: April 15, 1865

INAUGURATED AS PRESIDENT: March 4, 1861, age 52

KEY DATES:

1832   Serves as a soldier in the Black Hawk War against several groups of Native Americans.

1846   Elected to the House of Representatives.

1863   **JANUARY 1** Signs the Emancipation Proclamation.

1863   **NOVEMBER 19** Delivers the Gettysburg Address.

1865   **APRIL 9** Oversees the end of the Civil War after the south (Confederates) surrendered.

1865   **APRIL 14** Establishes the United States Secret Service to ensure the protection of national leaders. Ironically, he is assassinated the same day.

☞   Mary Lincoln **p130**

☞   The Civil War **pp160–61**

☞   Abolition of Slavery **pp162–63**

Abraham Lincoln

THE EMANCIPATION PROCLAMATION

On January 1, 1863, Lincoln issued the Emancipation Proclamation as a way of undermining the south. It declared all slaves in the breakaway Confederate states to be free, and allowed African Americans to join the Union army. Lincoln hoped this would increase his support among northern abolitionists and encourage slaves in the south to escape their owners and flee to the north.

LINCOLN AND SLAVERY

Lincoln expressed antislavery sentiments throughout his life, both in private and in public. Here he receives prominent antislavery campaigner Sojourner Truth into the White House in 1864, over a year after the Emancipation Proclamation was signed.

ASSASSINATION

On April 14, 1865, five days after the Civil War ended, Lincoln was enjoying a play at Ford's Theatre, in Washington, DC. During the third act, John Wilkes Booth, a Confederate supporter, sneaked into the private box where the president was seated and shot him in the back of his head. Lincoln was carried across the street to a boarding house, where he died the following morning.

DEATH AT THE THEATRE
Booth entered Lincoln's box while the presidential bodyguard was away. The single bullet he shot was fatal.

ANDREW JOHNSON

17th ★ 1865–1869

Democrat

Andrew Johnson had been vice president just six weeks when Lincoln was assassinated. Formerly a tailor before entering politics, he was a southerner who supported states' rights. This led him to be lenient toward the southern states during the Reconstruction period after the Civil War (which involved bringing the south back into the Union). However, the Republican-led Congress opposed this and managed to pass legislation protecting the rights of former slaves, overturning Johnson's veto on several occasions.

Johnson's **parents** were **illiterate** and it was **his wife** who **taught** him how to **read and write**.

DATA FILE

BORN: December 29, 1808, Raleigh, North Carolina
DIED: July 31, 1875

INAUGURATED AS PRESIDENT: April 15, 1865, age 56

KEY DATES:

1843   Elected to the House of Representatives.

1867   Sends Secretary of State William Seward to negotiate the purchase of Alaska from Russia.

1868   Acquitted in his impeachment trial.

☞   Abolition of Slavery **pp162–63**

IMPEACHMENT

Throughout his presidency, Johnson repeatedly clashed with the Republican-dominated Congress, leading them to pass several acts limiting his presidential powers. In 1867, Johnson defied one of these by removing the Secretary of War approved by the Senate and selecting his own candidate. Furious at his actions, the House of Representatives voted to impeach the president, which would bring formal charges against Johnson and could remove him from office. The trial went to the Senate, which eventually ruled in Johnson's favor by just one vote.

SERVING THE SUMMONS

Andrew Johnson was handed a summons on March 7, 1868, ordering him to appear before the Senate. He remains one of two presidents to be impeached by Congress, both of whom were later acquitted.

Andrew Johnson

ULYSSES S. GRANT

18th ★ 1869-1877 *Republican*

One of the Union's best generals in the Civil War, Ulysses S. Grant was renowned for leading the United States to victory over the Confederate states. A war hero from humble origins, his popularity helped him win the 1868 presidential election. However, he came into office during a difficult time in American history, faced with economic problems and the Reconstruction of the south. Grant favored mild measures to bring the last three states—Mississippi, Texas, and Virginia—back into the Union. However, he eventually threatened force against those states that denied the vote to African Americans. He was elected for a second term, but this was plagued by scandals, which tarnished his popularity.

DATA FILE

BORN: April 27, 1822, Point Pleasant, Ohio
DIED: July 23, 1885

INAUGURATED AS PRESIDENT:
March 4, 1869, age 46

KEY DATES:

1861 Volunteers his military services during the Civil War.

1870 Helps pass the 15th Amendment, which forbids denying rights to American citizens on the basis of their race.

☞ The Civil War **pp160–61**

☞ Voting Rights **pp164–65**

A **$50 bill** is **nicknamed** a **"Grant"** because it has his **portrait** on it.

THE PANIC OF 1873

In September 1873, Jay Cooke and Company, a bank with major investments in railroads, declared bankruptcy. This set off a series of other bank failures, and soon a major economic panic had swept the nation. Grant's policies were ineffective in stopping this and mass unemployment and strikes followed.

Ulysses S. Grant

RUTHERFORD B. HAYES

19th ★ **1877–1881**   *Republican*

Having served in the Civil War and as a state governor, Rutherford B. Hayes was a popular presidential candidate within his party. However, he took office after a highly contested election, only winning the presidency after a special commission ruled in his favor. As the president, he oversaw the final stage of Reconstruction and withdrew the federal army from the south. He had strained relations with Congress, which blocked his plans to reform the Civil Service.

DATA FILE

BORN: October 4, 1822, Delaware, Ohio
DIED: January 17, 1893

INAUGURATED AS PRESIDENT: March 4, 1877, age 55

KEY DATES:

1861   Serves in the Union army during the Civil War.

1877   Orders the last federal troops to leave the southern states.

1877   Issues an order barring all federal employees from political activity in an attempt to begin reforming the Civil Service.

☞ The Civil War **pp160–61**

☞ Extraordinary Elections **pp196–97**

In **1878**, Hayes **began** the tradition of the **Easter Egg roll** on the **White House lawn**.

THE CHINESE IMMIGRATION ACT

Chinese immigration to the US had been constant since the 1850s, with many immigrants working on the railroads. However, they were often resented because of the cheap labor they provided, and in 1879, Congress passed a bill forbidding all Chinese immigration. Hayes, however, vetoed the bill, which went against the terms of an earlier treaty with China. Instead, he negotiated a new agreement, which allowed immigration, but at a reduced rate.

DIPLOMATIC MEETING
President Hayes is shown here meeting Chinese diplomats during the negotiations for the new treaty.

Rutherford B. Hayes

JAMES A. GARFIELD

20th ★ 1881 Republican

A self-made man, James A. Garfield was the last US president to be born in a log cabin. His reputation as a Civil War hero earned him a seat in the House of Representatives, where he served nine terms. However, his presidency lasted only 200 days before he was assassinated. During his tenure, Garfield angered many in his party by trying to put an end to corruption, and also refusing to let the Senate choose his political appointments.

DATA FILE

BORN: November 19, 1831, Orange, Ohio
DIED: September 19, 1881

INAUGURATED AS PRESIDENT: March 4, 1881, age 49

KEY DATES:

1863 Promoted to major general for his bravery at the Battle of Chickamauga.

1881 Orders the investigation of corruption in the so-called Star Route scandal, where postal officials had received bribes for awarding profitable mail delivery contracts.

Garfield was the first **ambidextrous** president—he could **write with both hands**.

ASSASSINATION

Following his support of Civil Service reform, President Garfield was shot by Charles Guiteau, a disappointed office seeker, on July 2, 1881. The president was severely wounded and was taken back to the White House, where he underwent treatment for two months. The dirty instruments used to treat the wound caused blood poisoning, and Garfield died on September 19.

BITTER ATTACK

Garfield's attacker, Charles Guiteau, opened fire at the Baltimore and Potomac Railroad Station in Washington, DC, while the president was waiting for a train. Guiteau was quickly arrested after the shooting, and tried and hanged in June 1883.

James A. Garfield

CHESTER A. ARTHUR

21st ★ 1881-1885   *Republican*

The son of a Northern-Irish immigrant, Chester A. Arthur proved to be a surprisingly capable president when he assumed office after Garfield's assassination. For years he had benefited from the "spoils system," where political jobs were given to a party's supporters and friends, and Arthur was expected to pack his cabinet with his own supporters. However, he actually introduced reforms that increased the number of jobs awarded on merit.

Arthur was **very particular** about his **clothes** and allegedly **owned 80 pairs of trousers**.

DATA FILE

BORN: October 5, 1830, Fairfield, Vermont
DIED: November 18, 1886

INAUGURATED AS PRESIDENT:
September 20, 1881, age 50

KEY DATES:

1882   Signs the Chinese Exclusion Act forbidding immigration from China for 10 years.

1883   Proposes a reduction in tariffs on imports, but Congress adds so many exceptions to it that it becomes known as the "Mongrel Tariff" and is not very successful.

1883   Increases naval funds, so the navy can purchase its first steel vessels.

THE PENDLETON ACT

Until the 1880s, most Civil Service jobs were awarded on the basis of the "spoils system." However, this did not help government departments work efficiently, and in 1883, President Arthur signed the Pendleton Civil Service Reform Act into law. Often referred to as the "Pendleton Act" after its chief sponsor, Senator George Pendleton, this reform created an independent commission to oversee the Civil Service and introduced written examinations for those applying for top government jobs.

BITTERSWEET VICTORY

Although the act was championed by Democrat George Pendleton, it meant that Democrats would no longer be able to remove Republican office holders and replace them with their own. In this cartoon, Pendleton is congratulated by a Republican and realizes he has inadvertently helped his rival party.

THE FRIENDS OF THE BILL...

Chester A. Arthur

GROVER CLEVELAND

22nd/24th ★ 1885-1889/1893-1897 *Democrat*

A former governor of New York State, Grover Cleveland is the only president to have served two nonconsecutive terms, and was the first Democrat to be elected after the Civil War. In order to prevent Congress from enacting measures he did not support, Cleveland vetoed more legislation than any other president before him and also opposed foreign intervention. His second term was hit by an economic recession, which led to his falling popularity.

DATA FILE

BORN: March 18, 1837, Caldwell, New Jersey
DIED: June 24 1908

INAUGURATED AS PRESIDENT:
March 4, 1885, age 47
March 4, 1893, age 55

KEY DATES:

1886 Recommends that Congress accept the Statue of Liberty as a gift from France.

1893 Refuses to advance a treaty that would annex the Hawaii islands.

1893 Repeals the Sherman Silver Purchase Act. This act had required Congress to purchase a mandatory amount of silver each month and Cleveland blamed it for the recession.

 Frances Cleveland **p131**

Cleveland **paid** a **Polish immigrant $150** to fight in **his place** during the **Civil War**.

TAKING THE OATH
Cleveland, in the purple suit, places his hand on a Bible as he is sworn in for his first term in office.

THE PULLMAN STRIKE

In 1894, Chicago's Pullman railroad company reduced wages by 30 percent because of the economic crisis. This sparked a nationwide railroad strike that ended in violent outbreaks. Cleveland had to send in federal troops (as shown here) to restore order and end the strike.

Grover Cleveland

BENJAMIN
HARRISON

23rd ★ 1889–1893   *Republican*

The grandson of William Henry Harrison —the ninth president—Benjamin Harrison was a Civil War veteran with a reputation for honesty. During his tenure, he raised tariffs on imports to protect American goods, and also pursued an active foreign policy, submitting plans to annex Hawaii and organizing the first international conference of American states.

Harrison was the **first** president to have **electricity installed** in the **White House**.

DATA FILE

BORN: August 20, 1833, North Bend, Ohio
DIED: March 13, 1901

INAUGURATED AS PRESIDENT: March 4, 1889, age 55

KEY DATES:

1862   Volunteers for the Union army during the Civil War.

1881   Elected to the US Senate.

1890   Signs the McKinley Tariff Act to raise taxes on foreign imports.

ENTERING THE HARBOR

For many immigrants arriving from Europe, the Statue of Liberty was their first sight of the United States. On arrival, medical and legal inspections were held to determine if they were fit for entry into the country. Many who were suffering from infectious diseases were sent back to Europe.

ELLIS ISLAND

Until 1890, immigration policy was the responsibility of individual states. However, during Harrison's presidency the federal government took control. In 1892, a center at Ellis Island, New York City, was opened in which all new arrivals had to be processed. In the first year, 450,000 immigrants arrived, and over 12 million had passed through before Ellis Island was closed in 1954.

Benjamin Harrison

WILLIAM McKINLEY

25th ★ **1897-1901** *Republican*

After 14 years as a US representative, and eight as governor of Ohio, William McKinley aimed to protect the American economy by raising tariffs and linking the US dollar to the value of gold. However, his presidency was much more dominated by foreign affairs when the country became involved in the Spanish-American War. In 1901, six months into his second term, McKinley was assassinated by an anarchist.

DATA FILE

BORN: January 29, 1843, Niles, Ohio
DIED: September 14, 1901

INAUGURATED AS PRESIDENT: March 4, 1897, age 54

KEY DATES:

1897 Authorizes the Dingley Tariff Act, raising US tariffs to their highest levels.

1900 Sends US troops to China to help quell the Boxer Rebellion, where a group of Chinese nationalists had attacked Western missionaries and diplomats.

McKinley's **inauguration** in **1897** was the **first to be filmed**.

THE SPANISH-AMERICAN WAR

Cuba had begun fighting for independence from Spain in 1895 and reports of Spanish brutality against Cubans had stirred up calls for the United States to intervene. After a US battleship mysteriously blew up in Cuba in February 1898, McKinley agreed to go to war. US forces easily overcame the Spanish in Cuba, as well as winning naval battles across the Pacific, where other Spanish colonies were fighting for independence. In December, Spain was defeated and the Spanish government agreed to give Cuba its independence.

BATTLE OF MANILA BAY
US Marines watch from the shore as the Spanish fleet is defeated during a battle at Manila in the Philippines, on May 1, 1898. The first major engagement of the war, this battle was a decisive naval victory for the US.

William McKinley

THEODORE ROOSEVELT

26th ★ 1901-1909   *Republican*

Rising unexpectedly to the presidency after McKinley's assassination, Theodore Roosevelt proved to be an able and active leader whose determination to enact changes greatly enhanced the reputation of the presidential office. He clamped down hard on big businesses to stop their unfair practices, pushed for laws to improve the quality of America's food, and increased the number of national parks in the country. On the international front, he oversaw the building of the Panama Canal, and won the Nobel Peace Prize for negotiating the Treaty of Portsmouth, which ended the war between Russia and Japan.

A **boxing accident** left Roosevelt virtually **blind** in his **left eye**.

DATA FILE

BORN: October 27, 1858, New York, New York
DIED: January 6, 1919

INAUGURATED AS PRESIDENT: September 14, 1901, age 42

KEY DATES:

1898	Leads a volunteer cavalry regiment called the "Rough Riders" during the Spanish-American War.
1902	Orders action against the Northern Securities Company for unfairly restricting trade.
1906	**JUNE** Signs the Meat Inspection and Pure Food and Drug Acts, beginning government inspection of the food industry.
1906	**DECEMBER** Awarded the Nobel Peace Prize.

Theodore Roosevelt

THE PANAMA CANAL

The United States had long considered building a canal through Central America, which would connect the Atlantic and Pacific Oceans and provide an important shipping route for goods. However, progress was only made in 1902 when Roosevelt started negotiations with Colombia—which owned Panama—to buy land for this project. When the Colombians refused, the United States supported a revolution in Panama, which enabled it to declare its independence and then sell the land to the US. The construction of the canal lasted 10 years and cost $380 million.

PRESIDENTIAL VISIT
In November 1916, President Roosevelt visited the site of the canal himself. Here, he sits inside a digging machine.

CONSERVATION AND THE RECLAMATION ACT

Roosevelt's concern for the environment earned him the nickname "The Great Conservationist." Through the Reclamation Act of 1902, he secured funds from the sale of lands in the West to build dams to irrigate areas that were too dry for agriculture. Roosevelt also established the National Park Service and added 195,329 sq miles (505,900 sq km) to the national forests. In 1903, he established the first national wildlife refuge in Florida.

PROTECTING THE ENVIRONMENT
Roosevelt spent three days on a camping trip in Yosemite National Park with naturalist John Muir. During their trip, Muir persuaded the president to extend the boundaries that were under the park's protection.

Theodore Roosevelt

WILLIAM H. TAFT

27th ★ 1909-1913   *Republican*

Before becoming president, William H. Taft had gained wide experience as Solicitor General and governor of the Philippines. Trained as a lawyer, he had hoped for a place on the Supreme Court and was a reluctant presidential candidate. Upon taking office, he championed tariff reduction and employed "dollar diplomacy," a policy where the US provided loans to foreign countries in order to increase its overseas influence. With the admission of New Mexico and Arizona to the Union, he became the first president of the main 48 US states, known as the "contiguous 48."

THE PAYNE–ALDRICH ACT

Named after Senators Sereno E. Payne and Nelson W. Aldrich, the Payne-Aldrich Act was passed in 1909 to lower tariffs on goods entering the United States. However, the bill was weak, and lowered tariffs by only a very small percentage. Many Republicans were angered by Taft's support of it and this cartoon mocks the president, showing him greeting the "crippled" tariff bill.

THE FIRST PITCH

President Taft is shown here with his wife Helen at a baseball game in New York City. Taft began the custom of the president throwing the first pitch at the start of the professional season.

DATA FILE

BORN: September 15, 1857, Cincinnati, Ohio
DIED: March 8, 1930

INAUGURATED AS PRESIDENT: March 4, 1909, age 51

KEY DATES:

1890 Appointed US Solicitor General.

1901 Appointed governor of the Philippines.

1904 Appointed Secretary of War under Theodore Roosevelt.

1909 Signs the Payne-Aldrich Tariff Act.

At **330 pounds (150 kg)**, Taft was the **heaviest** president and had a **special bathtub** installed in the White House.

William H. Taft

WOODROW WILSON

28th ★ 1913–1921   *Democrat*

A former professor, Woodrow Wilson was a capable and determined president. A keen reformer, he pushed for lower tariffs and formed the Federal Trade Commission to clamp down on unfair business practices. Although he initially tried to stay out of foreign wars, when faced with German attacks on several US ships, Wilson took America into World War I. He later won the Nobel Peace Prize for his involvement in the post-war negotiations.

DATA FILE

BORN: December 28, 1856, Staunton, Virginia
DIED: February 3, 1924

INAUGURATED AS PRESIDENT: March 4, 1913, age 56

KEY DATES:

1890 Appointed as a professor of political science at Princeton University.

1917 Delivers a speech in the Senate urging the countries involved in World War I to opt for "peace without victory."

☞ Edith Wilson **p132**

☞ Prohibition **pp166–67**

☞ Female Suffrage **pp168–69**

Wilson kept a **flock of sheep** on the **White House lawn**.

THE TREATY OF VERSAILLES

Long before World War I ended, Wilson had drawn up proposals for an international peace settlement, known as the "Fourteen Points." These called for mild measures against the defeated countries and the establishment of a "League of Nations" to promote world peace. However, when the negotiations took place in Versailles, France, in 1919, the European leaders imposed much harsher terms on Germany than Wilson had hoped for. Back home, his plans also fell through when the Senate rejected the Treaty of Versailles and refused to join the League.

THE BIG FOUR

Most of the peace decisions were made by the Big Four nations: Italy, Britain, France, and the US. Here, their leaders, Vittorio Emanuele Orlando, David Lloyd George, Georges Clemenceau, and Wilson are pictured (seated, left to right) during the negotiations.

Woodrow Wilson

WARREN G. HARDING

29th ★ 1921–1923   *Republican*

Having made his fortune as a newspaper publisher, Warren G. Harding was a compromise choice as the Republican presidential candidate in 1920. His appeal for a "return to normalcy" after the war won him the election, but he proved to be a weak leader and was only able to push through a few major changes. He set rules for government spending by establishing the Bureau of the Budget in 1921, but suffered a series of corruption scandals during his time in office. He died suddenly in 1923, before these scandals had been brought to light.

DATA FILE

BORN: November 2, 1865, Corsica (now Blooming Grove), Ohio
DIED: August 2, 1923

INAUGURATED AS PRESIDENT: March 4, 1921, age 55

KEY DATES:

1914   Elected as a senator for Ohio.

1921   Signs the Budget and Accounting Act, which creates the Bureau of the Budget.

1921   Signs peace agreements with Germany, Austria, and Hungary, made necessary by the failure of the United States to ratify the Treaty of Versailles.

Harding was an **avid musician** and **played** the **alto horn** in a **brass band**.

THE WASHINGTON NAVAL CONFERENCE

After World War I, there were concerns that a buildup of naval power might lead to a new war. In 1921, Harding helped set up a conference in Washington, DC, to set limits on how many new warships could be built. Attended by nine nations, it was the first international conference held in the United States and resulted in a number of international agreements.

Warren G. Harding

CALVIN COOLIDGE

30th ★ 1923–1929 *Republican*

The son of a shopkeeper, Calvin Coolidge won public acclaim as governor of Massachusetts by boldly putting down a police strike in Boston. He became president after the sudden death of Harding in 1923, and restored faith in the office after the corruption scandals of the previous administration. A believer in minimal government interference, Coolidge governed with a light touch, vetoing many bills that he felt were too intrusive. He also kept the budget in check and cut income taxes, but failed to spot the economic warning signs that led to the stock market crash of 1929.

THE GREAT MISSISSIPPI FLOOD

The flooding of the Mississippi River in April 1926 was among the worst in US history. Coolidge was criticized for his slow response and for trying to block federal spending that could help the flood victims. More than 250 people died and thousands were left homeless.

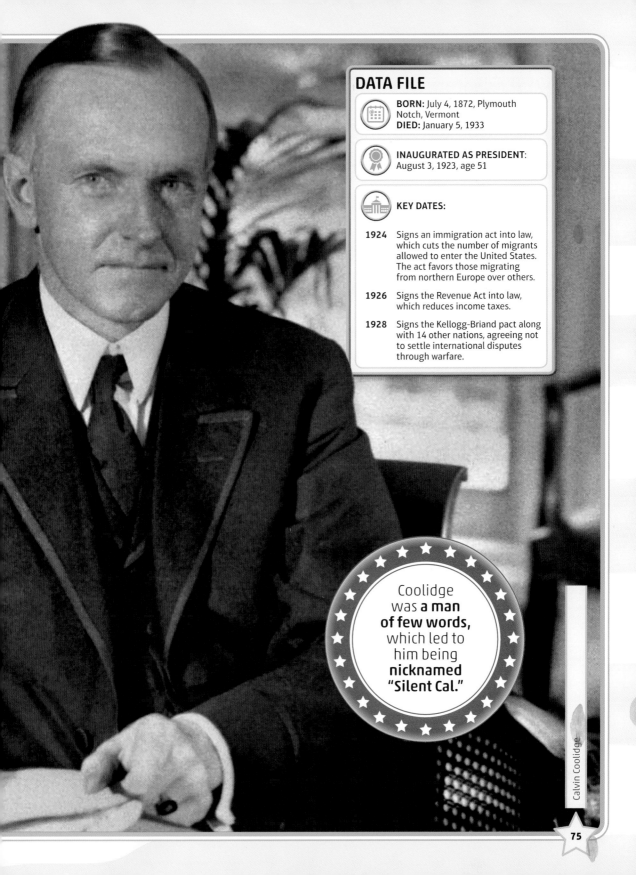

DATA FILE

BORN: July 4, 1872, Plymouth Notch, Vermont
DIED: January 5, 1933

INAUGURATED AS PRESIDENT: August 3, 1923, age 51

KEY DATES:

1924 Signs an immigration act into law, which cuts the number of migrants allowed to enter the United States. The act favors those migrating from northern Europe over others.

1926 Signs the Revenue Act into law, which reduces income taxes.

1928 Signs the Kellogg-Briand pact along with 14 other nations, agreeing not to settle international disputes through warfare.

Coolidge was **a man of few words,** which led to him being **nicknamed "Silent Cal."**

Calvin Coolidge

HERBERT HOOVER

31st ★ 1929-1933   *Republican*

Born into a Quaker family, Herbert Hoover made his fortune as a mining engineer. Before entering politics, he successfully organized a series of humanitarian efforts to provide food relief—achievements that made him a promising choice as president. However, just seven months after his inauguration, the stock market crashed. This led to the Great Depression, which blighted his presidency. Unemployment and poverty rose, and the measures Hoover took, such as lowering income tax, caused little relief.

DATA FILE

BORN: August 10, 1874, West Branch, Iowa
DIED: October 20, 1964

INAUGURATED AS PRESIDENT: March 4, 1929, age 54

KEY DATES:

1917 Heads the US Food Administration to help America through shortages of food imports during World War I.

1930 Raises tariffs to protect American farmers from foreign imports, but this sets off a trade war and makes the Depression worse.

 Lou Hoover **p133**

On October 29, 1929, the US stock market (on Wall Street, New York City) crashed, triggering a nationwide economic panic. Businesses failed, unemployment soared, and banks went bankrupt. Hoover did not believe it was the government's job to provide assistance for people, so many relied on soup kitchens, such as the one shown below.

WITH THE FIRST LADY
President Hoover is pictured here with his wife, Lou Hoover. He first met her at Stanford University, California, where she was the only female geology major.

Hoover was so **unpopular** during the **Depression** that **town slums** were nicknamed **"Hoovervilles."**

Herbert Hoover

FRANKLIN D.
ROOSEVELT

32nd ★ 1933–1945   *Democrat*

The longest-serving American president, Franklin D. Roosevelt won four terms in office and is remembered as one of the country's greatest leaders. Although crippled by polio in 1921, Roosevelt recovered and later became the governor of New York. He assumed the presidency during the Great Depression and introduced a range of programs to tackle the crisis, announcing to the nation "the only thing we have to fear is fear itself." Through his "New Deal" measures, Roosevelt helped the country recover, and, on the international front, he also led it ably through World War II.

DATA FILE

BORN: January 30, 1882, Hyde Park, New York
DIED: April 12, 1945

INAUGURATED AS PRESIDENT: March 4, 1933, age 51

KEY DATES:

1921 Struck by polio, which paralyzes his lower body.

1933 **MARCH** Signs the Emergency Banking Act, temporarily shutting down banks to stop panic withdrawals. This marks the start of his "100 days," in which numerous relief bills are passed.

1933 **DECEMBER** Oversees the end of Prohibition.

1945 Dies from bleeding in his brain three months into his fourth term.

☞ Eleanor Roosevelt **pp134–35**

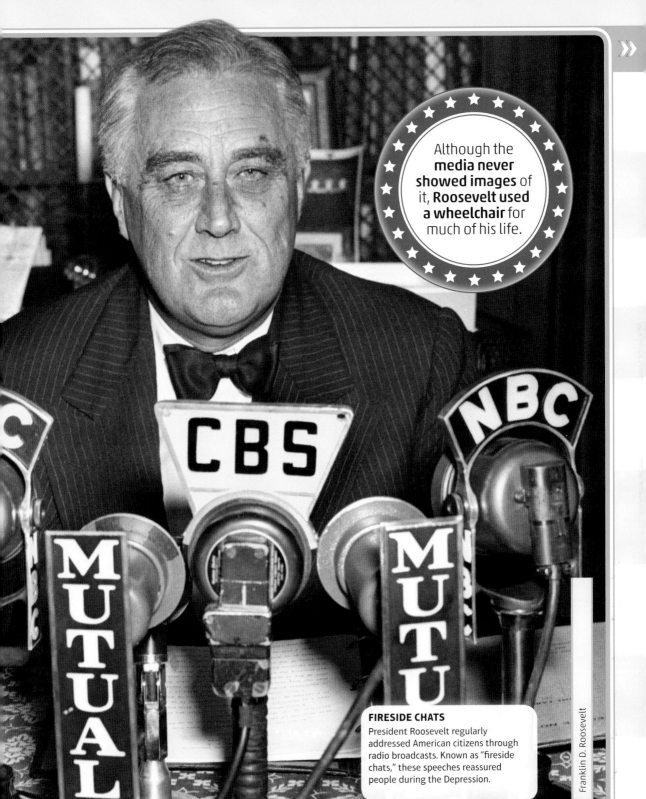

Although the **media never showed images** of it, **Roosevelt used a wheelchair** for much of his life.

FIRESIDE CHATS

President Roosevelt regularly addressed American citizens through radio broadcasts. Known as "fireside chats," these speeches reassured people during the Depression.

Franklin D. Roosevelt

THE NEW DEAL

The Great Depression left 15 million people unemployed, something Roosevelt promised to address with a "New Deal" for Americans. As well as providing direct grants to the states so they could support their unemployed citizens, he set up a variety of federal programs to create jobs, including projects to build roads and plant trees. These initiatives benefited many people and helped the American economy grow.

RELIEF PROGRAMS
Roosevelt's work programs helped feed thousands of Americans. In this image, workers on a New Deal project in New York City receive a free meal.

PEARL HARBOR

Roosevelt's pledge to keep the United States out of World War II ended on December 7, 1941, when the Japanese launched a surprise bombing attack on the US naval base at Pearl Harbor. President Roosevelt declared war on Japan and its allies the next day. Over the next few years, Roosevelt gradually committed more troops to the war, leading to an eventual victory.

The **Japanese attack** at Pearl Harbor **lasted 110 minutes**.

HEAVY CASUALTIES

Smoke rises up from the *USS Arizona* after it was struck by Japanese bomber planes. In total, 2,400 American servicemen were killed and 19 ships destroyed in the Pearl Harbor attack.

Franklin D. Roosevelt

81

HARRY S. TRUMAN

33rd ★ 1945–1953 *Democrat*

A former haberdasher from Missouri, Harry S. Truman became president after Franklin D. Roosevelt's sudden death in 1945. As he led America through the last months of World War II, he faced huge challenges and made the difficult decision to drop nuclear bombs on Japan. Truman's presidency marked the beginning of the Cold War between the United States and the communist Soviet Union, where tensions grew between the two countries. Truman took several actions to prevent the influence of Soviet communism in other countries, a policy that was known as the Truman Doctrine.

THE ATOMIC BOMB

After the US successfully created an atomic bomb in May 1945, Truman decided to use this to bring an end to the war with Japan. In August that year, nuclear bombs were dropped on the Japanese cities of Nagasaki and Hiroshima. These caused a devastating impact and around 200,000 people died. Soon after, Japan surrendered.

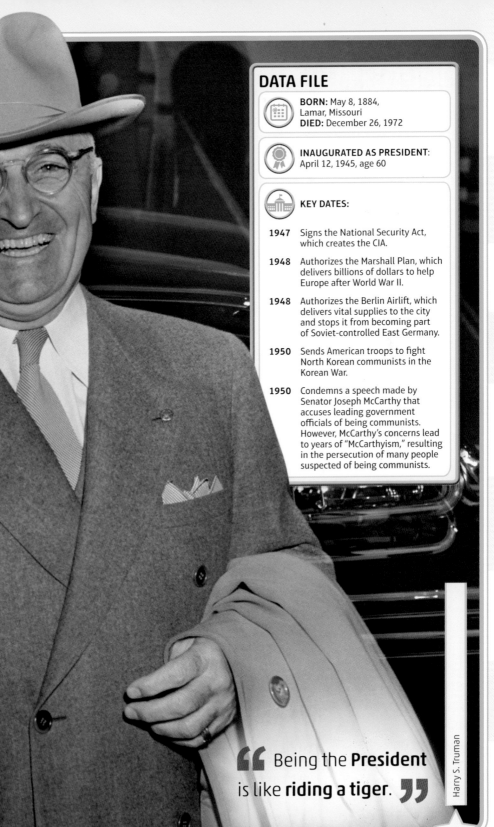

DATA FILE

BORN: May 8, 1884, Lamar, Missouri
DIED: December 26, 1972

INAUGURATED AS PRESIDENT:
April 12, 1945, age 60

KEY DATES:

1947 Signs the National Security Act, which creates the CIA.

1948 Authorizes the Marshall Plan, which delivers billions of dollars to help Europe after World War II.

1948 Authorizes the Berlin Airlift, which delivers vital supplies to the city and stops it from becoming part of Soviet-controlled East Germany.

1950 Sends American troops to fight North Korean communists in the Korean War.

1950 Condemns a speech made by Senator Joseph McCarthy that accuses leading government officials of being communists. However, McCarthy's concerns lead to years of "McCarthyism," resulting in the persecution of many people suspected of being communists.

❝ Being the **President** is like **riding a tiger**. ❞

Harry S. Truman

DWIGHT D. EISENHOWER

34th ★ 1953-1961   *Republican*

A military hero, Dwight D. Eisenhower commanded several missions during World War II. Although he had no political experience, he won an easy victory when he ran for the presidency, promising to pursue a strong foreign policy. Once in office, Eisenhower struggled to contain communist expansion in Asia and the Middle East, while avoiding open war. He also tried to improve relations with the Soviet Union and set up the first superpower summit. Even though he suffered from health problems during his second term, the country's strong economic growth ensured his good reputation.

Nicknamed Ike, Eisenhower used the **successful campaign slogan "I like Ike"** to get elected.

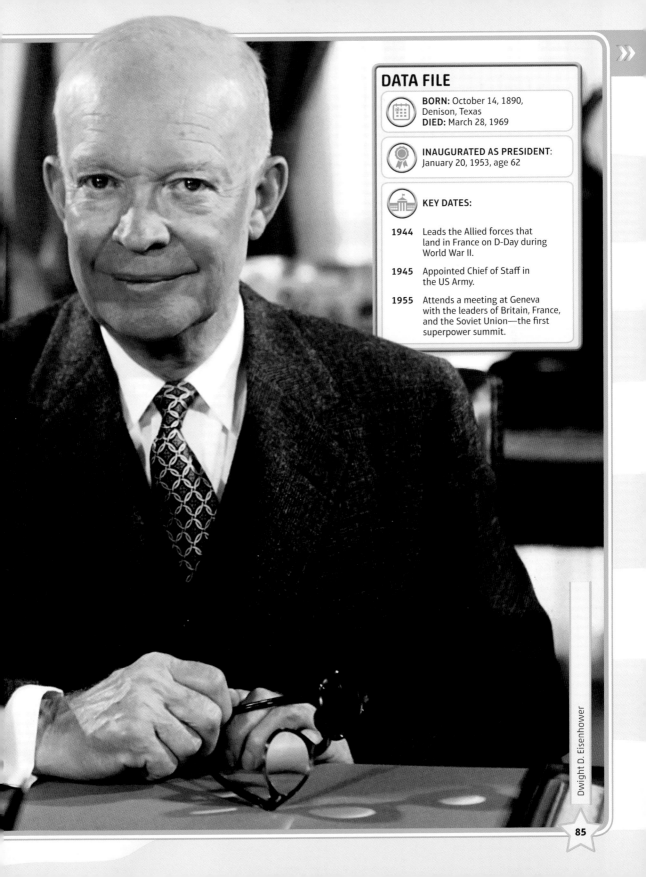

DATA FILE

BORN: October 14, 1890, Denison, Texas
DIED: March 28, 1969

INAUGURATED AS PRESIDENT:
January 20, 1953, age 62

KEY DATES:

1944 Leads the Allied forces that land in France on D-Day during World War II.

1945 Appointed Chief of Staff in the US Army.

1955 Attends a meeting at Geneva with the leaders of Britain, France, and the Soviet Union—the first superpower summit.

Dwight D. Eisenhower

CIVIL RIGHTS

In many southern US states, education had remained segregated well into the 1950s, with African American and white children attending separate schools. In 1954, the Supreme Court declared this unconstitutional and ordered schools to desegregate immediately. However, when the school board at Little Rock, Arkansas, announced these plans, the Arkansas governor called in the National Guard to prevent black students from entering the high school. Eisenhower was forced to send federal troops to grant them access.

HOSTILE WELCOME

Elizabeth Eckford was one of the nine black students to attempt to enter the Central High School at Little Rock, Arkansas, on September 4, 1957. Pictured here, she faces angry crowds trying to block her entry.

The **first "astronaut"** of Project Mercury was a **rhesus monkey** called **Sam**.

THE SPACE RACE

In October 1957, the United States suffered a shock when the Soviet Union announced the launch of Sputnik 1, the first satellite, into space, starting a "space race" between the two superpowers. On January 31, 1958, the first US satellite, Explorer I, was launched. Later that year, Eisenhower created the National Aeronautics and Space Administration (NASA), with the task of sending an American astronaut into space.

PROJECT MERCURY

Launched in 1958, Project Mercury aimed to send an American into space before the Soviet Union made its own manned space flight. In 1961, Soviet astronaut Yuri Gagarin became the first man in space, followed just three weeks later by the first American, Alan Shepard (pictured top left).

Dwight D. Eisenhower

JOHN F. KENNEDY

35th ★ 1961–1963   *Democrat*

A charismatic leader, John F. Kennedy was the youngest president ever elected. During his presidency, he pursued an active foreign policy, authorizing the use of military force to try to stop the spread of communism in Cuba and Vietnam. As Cold War tensions grew, he also convinced the Soviet Union to sign the Nuclear Test Ban Treaty, which limited the testing of nuclear weapons. At home, he promoted civil rights and sent troops to universities in the south to stop the racial segregation of students.

PRESIDENTIAL CAMPAIGN
As an attractive young couple, Kennedy and his wife Jackie appealed to many voters. Here they wave to crowds during a ticker-tape parade through New York City.

Presidents

DATA FILE

BORN: May 29, 1917, Brookline, Massachusetts
DIED: November 22, 1963

INAUGURATED AS PRESIDENT: January 20, 1961, age 43

KEY DATES:

1961   **MARCH** Establishes the Peace Corps, a volunteer program for US citizens to provide aid to underdeveloped countries.

1961   **APRIL** Authorizes the invasion of Cuba by CIA-trained Cuban exiles. The invasion fails and Kennedy has to negotiate to get the prisoners released.

1961   **MAY** Announces to Congress the goal to put a man on the Moon.

1963   **JUNE** Delivers a famous speech on civil rights, proposing a bill that was later passed by his successor, Lyndon B. Johnson.

1963   **JULY** Signs the Nuclear Test Ban Treaty with the Soviet Union.

1963   **NOVEMBER** Killed by an assassin at just 46 years old.

☞ Jacqueline Kennedy **p136**

> Ask not what **your country can do** for you—ask **what you can do** for your country.
>
> John F. Kennedy, Inaugural Address, 1961

John F. Kennedy

NUCLEAR THREAT
Taken by American spy planes, aerial photographs such as this one showed the presence of missile equipment in Cuba, and would have been among the evidence presented to Kennedy.

During the crisis, **officials pretended Kennedy had a cold** to explain why he did not appear in public.

THE CUBAN MISSILE CRISIS

In October 1962, US intelligence agencies found evidence that the Soviet Union was building nuclear missile bases in nearby Cuba. Since this severely threatened the security of the United States, Kennedy demanded that the bases be demolished and any missiles withdrawn. He then ordered a naval blockade of Cuba to stop Soviet ships from going to the island. As the US and the Soviet Union confronted each other, the world came close to a nuclear war. Finally, after a 13-day stand-off, the Soviet leader Nikita Khrushchev backed down and agreed to remove the missiles from Cuba.

ASSASSINATION

On November 22, 1963, Kennedy traveled to Dallas, Texas, to campaign for the 1964 elections. As the president rode through the city, an assassin opened fire, killing Kennedy almost immediately. This brutal murder of the young president was a tragedy that shocked the world. Lee Harvey Oswald was arrested for the murder, but he himself was shot dead two days later. Oswald's reasons for assassinating Kennedy have remained unclear, and many people claim the assassination was part of a wider conspiracy.

A FATAL RIDE
When he was killed, Kennedy was traveling in an open limousine with his wife, Jackie. They were accompanied by Texas governor John Connally, who was also wounded in the shooting.

John F. Kennedy

LYNDON B. JOHNSON

36th ★ 1963–1969   *Democrat*

Having served in both the House of Representatives and the Senate, Lyndon B. Johnson unexpectedly became president after John F. Kennedy's assassination. His dream was to build a "Great Society" through education and welfare reforms. As well as passing legislation to tackle poverty, Johnson promoted measures to bar racial discrimination in employment and to ensure voting rights for African Americans. However, US involvement in the Vietnam War increased during his presidency, which caused him to leave office unpopular.

ELECTION CAMPAIGN

Johnson is shown here addressing a campaign rally during the 1964 presidential election. He won by a wide margin, defeating his opponent Barry Goldwater.

DATA FILE

BORN: August 27, 1908, Stonewall, Texas
DIED: January 22, 1973

INAUGURATED AS PRESIDENT: November 22, 1963, age 55

KEY DATES:

1964   Signs the Civil Rights Act.

1964   Signs the Economic Opportunity Act, beginning his "war on poverty."

1965   **JULY 28** Authorizes sending American troops to Vietnam. The numbers increase rapidly to 400,000 by the end of 1966.

1965   **JULY 30** Signs Medicaid and Medicare into law, which provide hospital and medical insurance for poor and elderly Americans.

☞   "Lady Bird" Johnson **p137**

Johnson was the **first** to take the **presidential oath** on board a **plane**.

Lyndon B. Johnson

THE CIVIL RIGHTS ACT

Although slavery had been abolished and African Americans had been given voting rights, discrimination against them remained deep-rooted, especially in the south. To help address this, in 1964 Johnson signed the Civil Rights Act, which outlawed segregation in hotels, restaurants, and other public places. It also made it illegal for employers to discriminate on the grounds of color. Johnson later followed this with the Voting Rights Act in 1965, which banned a range of practices, such as literacy tests, which had been used to prevent African Americans from voting.

SIGNING THE ACT
Johnson helped pass numerous pieces of legislation to fulfill his vision of making the US a "Great Society." Here, the president shakes hands with the civil rights activist Dr. Martin Luther King Jr. at the official signing of the Civil Rights Act.

THE VIETNAM WAR

Conflict in Vietnam had been ongoing since 1954, as the South Vietnamese government tried to fight off the communist forces of the Vietcong, who were supported by North Vietnam. The US had previously sent military advisors, but in 1964 Johnson made the decision to also send armed troops, and to bomb bases in North Vietnam and Cambodia. The numbers of US soldiers grew steadily, from 3,500 in 1964 to 550,000 in 1968. As American casualties mounted, there were huge antiwar demonstrations across America and, in March 1968, Johnson agreed to reduce the US presence in Vietnam.

TRANSPORTING TROOPS
Helicopters played an important role in transporting US troops to combat zones in Vietnam. The US forces were unused to the difficult terrain and suffered heavy losses during the fighting.

Lyndon B. Johnson

RICHARD M. NIXON

37th ★ 1969–1974   *Republican*

A sharp and determined political operator, Richard M. Nixon had served as Dwight D. Eisenhower's vice president before being elected to the presidency in 1968. Foreign policy dominated the first part of his presidency; he reduced the number of American troops in Vietnam and negotiated an end to the war, as well as signing an important arms control agreement with the Soviet Union. Nixon was also the first US president to visit China. At home, he took measures to control inflation, but his career was destroyed by the Watergate scandal and ended in his resignation.

Nixon is the **only president** to have **resigned**.

DATA FILE

📅 **BORN:** January 9, 1913,
Yorba Linda, California
DIED: April 22, 1994

🎖️ **INAUGURATED AS PRESIDENT:**
January 20, 1969, age 56

🏛️ **KEY DATES:**

1970 Establishes the Environmental
Protection Agency to monitor
and control pollution.

1971 Freezes wages and prices
for 90 days in an attempt
to reduce inflation.

1972 **FEBRUARY** Visits China to
establish diplomatic relations
between the two countries.

1972 **MAY** Signs the SALT agreement
with the Soviet Union, which
limits the number of nuclear
missiles each country is allowed
to possess.

Richard M. Nixon

LUNAR LANDING
This image shows Buzz Aldrin (the second man on the Moon), photographed by Neil Armstrong. The two astronauts spent about two hours on the Moon's surface and left an American flag there.

" For **every American**, this has to be the **proudest day of their lives**. "
Nixon describing the Moon landing

THE FIRST MAN ON THE MOON

In 1961, President Kennedy had announced the goal of landing a person on the Moon within a decade, with the National Aeronautics and Space Administration (NASA) setting up the Apollo program to achieve this. On July 20, 1969, the Apollo 11 mission reached the Moon and astronaut Neil Armstrong became the first man to set foot on its surface. The historic event was televised and Nixon spoke to the astronauts via a radio link to congratulate them.

THE WATERGATE SCANDAL

In 1972, during Nixon's reelection campaign, several men broke into the Democratic National Committee's headquarters at the Watergate Hotel. Investigations into the burglary revealed that senior Republicans had tried to secretly record the Democrat campaign and had engaged in other illegal acts against their opponents. Nixon denied responsibility, but an audio recording system in Nixon's White House office revealed a coverup. When the Senate threatened to impeach him in July 1974, Nixon resigned.

IMPEACH NIXON
Demonstrators call for the impeachment of Nixon in October 1973. If the president had not resigned, he would have faced a trial by the Senate and almost certain dismissal.

Richard M. Nixon

GERALD R.
FORD
38th ★ 1974-1977 *Republican*

Gerald R. Ford rose to the office of president after Richard M. Nixon resigned over the Watergate Affair. A football star and law school graduate, Ford had earned a reputation for integrity during his many years of service in Congress. However, he soon lost his popularity after granting a "full, free, and absolute pardon" to Nixon. During his short term in office, he struggled to solve America's twin economic problems of rising inflation and unemployment. Overseas, Ford presided over the final stages of America's withdrawal from Vietnam.

DATA FILE

BORN: July 14, 1913, Omaha, Nebraska
DIED: December 26, 2006

INAUGURATED AS PRESIDENT:
August 9, 1974, age 61

KEY DATES:

1973   Becomes vice president after Spiro T. Agnew resigns over accusations of income tax fraud.

1974   Pardons former president Nixon.

1974   Forms the Economic Policy Board to provide advice to the president on financial issues.

1975   Escapes two assassination attempts.

☞   Betty Ford **p138**

Presidents

Ford is the **only president** who was **never elected** to the office of **president or vice president**.

THE FALL OF SAIGON

By 1975, the Vietcong Communist army had captured most of South Vietnam and were preparing to invade the city of Saigon. Many South Vietnamese troops fled by boat, but President Ford also ordered a massive airlift operation to rescue Americans and other civilians. This event marked the end of the Vietnam War.

Gerald R. Ford

JIMMY CARTER

39th ★ 1977–1981   Democrat

A native Georgian, Carter grew up on a peanut farm owned by his father. He took office at a difficult time and despite promoting many social reforms, rising unemployment and inflation dented his reputation. Abroad, Carter pursued a compassionate foreign policy, pushing for human rights and negotiating peace treaties. However, his presidency also saw the renewal of Cold War tensions with the Soviet Union after the Soviet army invaded Afghanistan in 1979. The end of his term was overshadowed by the Iran hostage crisis, when militant students in Tehran held American diplomats hostage for over a year and Carter struggled to gain their release.

THE CAMP DAVID ACCORDS

In September 1978, Carter invited Egyptian President Anwar Sadat (left) and Israeli Prime Minister Menachem Begin (right) to the presidential retreat at Camp David. They signed a historic agreement thirteen days later, bringing about peace between their two countries for the first time since 1947.

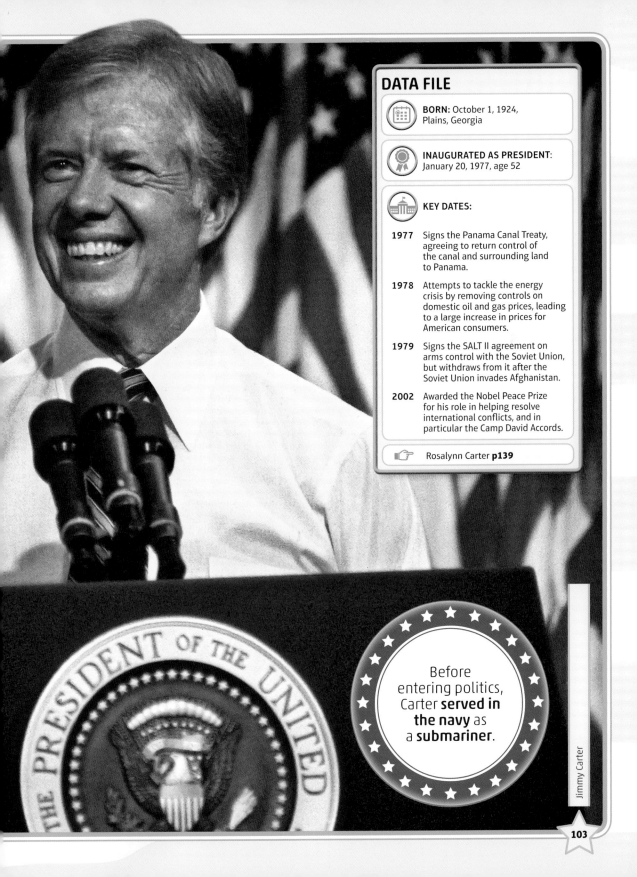

DATA FILE

BORN: October 1, 1924, Plains, Georgia

INAUGURATED AS PRESIDENT: January 20, 1977, age 52

KEY DATES:

1977 Signs the Panama Canal Treaty, agreeing to return control of the canal and surrounding land to Panama.

1978 Attempts to tackle the energy crisis by removing controls on domestic oil and gas prices, leading to a large increase in prices for American consumers.

1979 Signs the SALT II agreement on arms control with the Soviet Union, but withdraws from it after the Soviet Union invades Afghanistan.

2002 Awarded the Nobel Peace Prize for his role in helping resolve international conflicts, and in particular the Camp David Accords.

☞ Rosalynn Carter **p139**

Before entering politics, Carter **served in the navy** as a **submariner**.

Jimmy Carter

RONALD REAGAN

40th ★ 1981-1989 *Republican*

Known as the "Great Communicator," Ronald Reagan began his career as a film actor before going on to serve eight years as the governor of California. He survived an assassination attempt early in his presidency, and then spent most of his first term implementing "Reaganomics"—a program of reducing taxes and cutting back on welfare programs. However, when the economy went into a downturn, government debt increased to more than $2 trillion. Despite this setback, Reagan remained an extremely popular president.

DATA FILE

BORN: February 6, 1911, Tampico, Illinois
DIED: June 5, 2004

INAUGURATED AS PRESIDENT:
January 20, 1981, age 69

KEY DATES:

1981 Appoints the first female justice, Sandra Day O'Connor, to the Supreme Court.

1984 Reelected for a second term, with the second-largest victory margin in the 20th century.

1985 Signs the Gramm-Rudman Hollings Act, which attempts to control the government's growing debt.

☞ Nancy Reagan **p140**

Reagan was an **anticommunist informer** for the **FBI** in Hollywood in the **1940s**.

Ronald Reagan

THE LEADERS MEET
Pictured here in November 1985, Reagan and Mikhail Gorbachev meet during the American-Soviet summit in Geneva. These meetings began to ease longstanding tensions between the two countries.

SUMMITS WITH GORBACHEV

Relations with the Soviet Union were very strained in the early years of Reagan's presidency. He ordered the creation of the Strategic Defense Initiative ("Star Wars"), a project to shoot down Soviet missiles if they attacked the US. However, when Mikhail Gorbachev, the new Soviet leader, promised reform in 1985, Reagan reached out to him. They signed the Intermediate-Range Nuclear Forces Treaty in 1987, agreeing to limit their nuclear weapons.

THE IRAN-CONTRA AFFAIR

In 1986, it was revealed that members of Reagan's government were secretly selling weapons to Iran to gain the release of American hostages in Lebanon. This caused a scandal, as Reagan had publicly opposed selling arms to Iran. Additionally, the profit from these sales was being sent to the Contras—opponents of the communist regime in Nicaragua—support for whom was banned by Congress. Investigations took place but the extent of Reagan's involvement remained unclear.

CONGRESSIONAL HEARINGS

A congressional committee held televised hearings to get to the bottom of the scandal. Here, Lieutenant Colonel Oliver North, one of several key figures involved in the affair, testifies before the committee.

Ronald Reagan

GEORGE H. W. BUSH

41st ★ **1989–1993** *Republican*

A former Texas oil man, George H. W. Bush was Ronald Reagan's vice president for eight years. His presidency was dominated by foreign affairs, including the challenges caused by the collapse of the Soviet Union, and the Gulf War, which broke out when Iraq invaded Kuwait. At home, he passed measures to cut government debt, but his support of tax increases and growing unemployment cost him reelection.

DATA FILE

BORN: June 12, 1924, Milton, Massachusetts

INAUGURATED AS PRESIDENT: January 20, 1989, age 64

KEY DATES:

1989 Sends US forces into Panama to capture its president, who was suspected of involvement in drug trafficking.

1990 Signs the Americans with Disabilities Act, which makes it illegal for employers to discriminate based on disability.

1990 Sends US troops to expel Iraqi forces in Kuwait.

☞ Barbara Bush **p141**

Bush became **hard of hearing** after **piloting** noisy **bomber aircraft** during **World War II**.

Presidents

THE FALL OF THE BERLIN WALL

After World War II, Germany had been divided into communist East Germany (supported by the Soviet Union) and capitalist West Germany (supported by the US). In 1989, after demonstrations against its government, East Germany allowed people to cross the Berlin Wall, which had formerly prevented free movement between the two sides of the country. This symbolic event marked the end of the Cold War, and led to the eventual reunification of Germany in October 1990, which President Bush helped negotiate.

THE WALL COMES DOWN

On November 9, 1989, an announcement that East Germans could travel freely to the West led to thousands crossing the Berlin Wall, which divided the two halves of the city. Many took to knocking down parts of the wall themselves, while others celebrated by climbing on top of the wall.

George H. W. Bush

109

BILL
CLINTON
42nd ★ 1993-2001 *Democrat*

The youthful image of William J. Clinton (known as Bill) and his promises to reform healthcare and balance the budget meant his presidency began with a sense of hope. During his first term, he achieved much abroad with his involvement in peace deals in Northern Ireland, Bosnia, and the Middle East, and at home he presided over a time of prosperity. However, when the Democrats lost control of both houses of Congress, his healthcare reforms were watered down. Although he remained popular, the end of his presidency was overshadowed by personal scandals.

In **high school**, Clinton **played** in a **jazz band** called **Three Blind Mice**.

Presidents

DATA FILE

BORN: August 19, 1946, Hope, Arkansas

INAUGURATED AS PRESIDENT: January 20, 1993, age 46

KEY DATES:

1978   Elected governor of Arkansas.

1994   Signs an agreement that establishes the General Agreement on Tariffs and Trade (GATT), the body that regulates world trade.

1995   Clashes with the Republican-led Congress on how best to balance the budget. This leads to a temporary government shutdown.

1995   Visits Northern Ireland, where he plays a key role in bringing about the historic Good Friday agreement, which ended 30 years of conflict between different political groups.

1998   Impeachment proceedings brought against him due to his having lied about having an affair with a White House intern. He is later acquitted.

☞   Hillary Clinton **p142**

WINNING TWO TERMS

Clinton was reelected in the 1996 presidential race, even though the Republicans had gained control of Congress in 1994. He was the first Democrat to win two terms since Franklin D. Roosevelt.

Bill Clinton

THE WORLD TRADE CENTER BOMBING

On February 26, 1993, a bomb explosion ripped through the World Trade Center building in New York, killing six people and injuring a thousand more. The bomber, Ramzi Yousef, was part of a network of Middle Eastern terrorists who left explosives in a garage in the building's basement. Yousef was later captured in Pakistan and sentenced to life imprisonment. Clinton condemned the attack amid calls for improved security measures in government buildings.

EVACUATION OPERATION
Following the bombing, many people were trapped in the elevators when the power failed. In this image, fire crews can be seen working to rescue employees.

The **homemade bomb** that **exploded weighed** around **1,200 pounds** (544.3 kilograms).

THE WYE RIVER SUMMIT

Conflict between Arabs and Jewish settlers in Palestine—which had been ongoing since the 19th century—worsened after the establishment of Israel in 1947, and attempts at peace met with little success. In 1998, Clinton intervened and invited Israeli Prime Minister Benjamin Netanyahu and Palestinian leader Yasser Arafat for peace talks near Wye Mills, Maryland. He secured an agreement that Palestine would recognize Israel's right to exist and try to stop terrorist attacks against it. In turn, Israel would transfer some territory to Palestine. However, there have been outbreaks of fighting between the two sides ever since.

PEACE NEGOTIATIONS

King Hussein of Jordan (second from left), watches with President Clinton as Palestine Liberation Organization Chairman Yasser Arafat (far left) and Israeli Prime Minister Benjamin Netanyahu (far right) greet each other. Both Hussein and Clinton played a key role in helping bring about the agreement.

Bill Clinton

GEORGE W.
BUSH

43rd ★ 2001-2009   *Republican*

The son of a former president, George W. Bush worked in the family oil business before entering politics. He won the 2000 presidential race by a very narrow margin, but went on to serve two full terms in office. Bush's presidency was largely defined by the 9/11 terrorist attacks, after which he declared a "War on Terror." As part of this, he sent US troops to Afghanistan to dismantle the terrorist organization al-Qaeda, and to Iraq to overthrow the dictator Saddam Hussein.

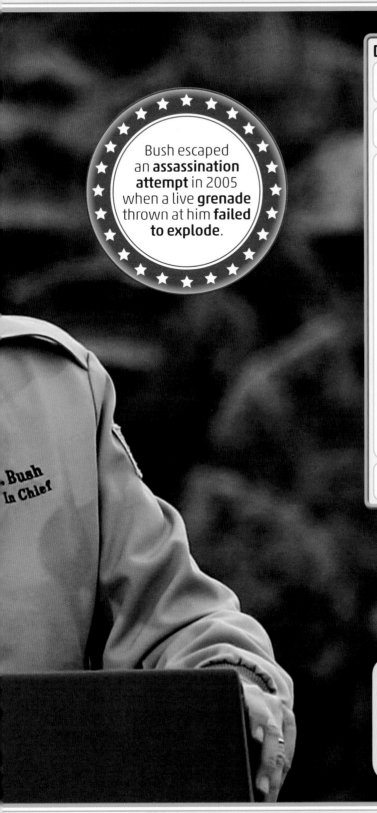

Bush escaped an **assassination attempt** in 2005 when a live **grenade** thrown at him **failed to explode**.

. Bush
In Chief

DATA FILE

BORN: July 6, 1946, New Haven, Connecticut

INAUGURATED AS PRESIDENT: January 20, 2001, age 54

KEY DATES:

2001 **MARCH** Withdraws support from the Kyoto Protocol, which commits participating countries to reducing their greenhouse gas emissions in order to help prevent global warming.

2001 **MAY** Signs a law approving a $1.35 trillion package of tax cuts. As a result, the government debt increases.

2001 **OCTOBER** Signs the Patriot Act, which gives increased powers to government agencies to carry out surveillance.

2001 **OCTOBER** Launches military action in Afghanistan.

2002 Signs into law the No Child Left Behind Act, which introduces new testing measures and makes schools more accountable for the progress of their students.

☞ Laura Bush **p143**

☞ Extraordinary Elections **pp196–97**

BUSH AND THE MARINES
President Bush speaks to US Marines at Camp Pendleton on December 7, 2004—the 63rd anniversary of the Japanese attack on Pearl Harbor. During his time in office, Bush significantly increased spending on defense.

George W. Bush

THE TWIN TOWERS
Smoke and flames can be seen pouring out of the two World Trade Center towers, moments after they were hit by the two aircraft. The large-scale attack shocked people around the world.

THE 9/11 TERROR ATTACKS

On September 11, 2001, members of the al-Qaeda terrorist group hijacked four passenger planes. They flew the first plane into the North Tower of the World Trade Center in New York and, 15 minutes later, the second plane into the South Tower. Both collapsed within two hours, killing more than 3,000 people. The third plane was piloted into the Pentagon, the headquarters of the US Department of Defense in Virginia, and the fourth crashed in a field after the passengers tried to take back control. These horrific acts of terrorism devastated America. Bush responded by announcing a "War on Terror" and created the Department of Homeland Security to tackle such threats.

THE IRAQ WAR

In 2002, Bush accused the Iraqi government—led by Saddam Hussein—of developing chemical and nuclear weapons. Although United Nations inspectors found no clear evidence of these weapons, the US, and a coalition of allies, invaded Iraq in 2003. US troops took control of the capital, Baghdad, on April 9, and removed Hussein's government, but this led to violence between different religious sects. The ensuing efforts to stabilize Iraq lasted for many years. By 2016, more than 4,800 American soldiers had died and the war had become very controversial.

PREPARING TO INVADE
US armored forces move into position on the Kuwait-Iraq border, two days ahead of the invasion of Iraq in March 2003.

BARACK
OBAMA

44th ★ **2009–2017** *Democrat*

A constitutional law professor and Illinois senator, Barack Obama was the first African American to be elected president. In his first term, he passed measures to reduce the impact of the global economic crisis of 2008, to introduce affordable federally funded healthcare, and to withdraw American troops from Afghanistan and Iraq. Obama continued to be active abroad during his second term and made a deal with Iran to limit its nuclear activities. Due to the continuing threat of global terrorism, he sent US forces to help stop the spread of the terrorist organization Islamic State in Iraq and Syria.

CONFIDENT STATESMAN

A charismatic leader, President Obama is pictured here greeting schoolchildren assembled on the South Lawn of the White House. In the 2008 election, he promoted a message of hope and change, inspiring many to vote for him.

Obama has **won two Grammy Awards**, for spoken word **narrations of his books**.

DATA FILE

BORN: August 4, 1961, Honolulu, Hawaii

INAUGURATED AS PRESIDENT: January 20, 2009, age 47

KEY DATES:

2009 Signs the American Recovery and Reinvestment Act, to help the US economy recover from the global economic crisis.

2011 **MAY** Informs the nation that a team of US Navy Seals has killed the terrorist leader Osama bin Laden in Abbottabad, Pakistan.

2011 **DECEMBER** Finishes withdrawing American troops from Iraq.

2014 Orders airstrikes against Islamic State positions in Iraq.

2015 Announces that around 5,000 troops will stay on in Afghanistan.

☞ Michelle Obama **pp144–45**

THE AFFORDABLE HEALTHCARE FOR AMERICA ACT

Past attempts to provide federal funding for healthcare had always failed or been vetoed. After a 2000 World Health Organization report placed the US 37th in global healthcare rankings, Obama put forth measures to improve this, which became known as "Obamacare." These became law in March 2010, and made individual health insurance compulsory for those not covered by their employers, as well as creating federal subsidies for health insurance for the poor.

DOCTORS FOR OBAMA
Supporters of Obama's Affordable Care Act, known as ACA or Obamacare, rally outside the Supreme Court in June 2015. The court ruled against a claim that some elements of the act were unconstitutional.

IMPROVED RELATIONS WITH CUBA

Relations between the US and Cuba had been strained since 1959. After Fidel Castro's communist government came to power, the US had broken off diplomatic and business ties with Cuba. In 2015, Obama sought to remedy this situation. He removed Cuba from a list of countries that sponsor terrorism, made it easier for Americans to travel there, reopened the US embassy in Havana, and in 2016, became the first US president to visit the island since 1928.

HAND OF FRIENDSHIP
Obama greets Cuban president Raúl Castro at the United Nations in September 2015—a symbol of the thaw in Cuban-American relations after nearly 60 years of tension.

Barack Obama

DONALD TRUMP

45th ★ 2017   *Republican*

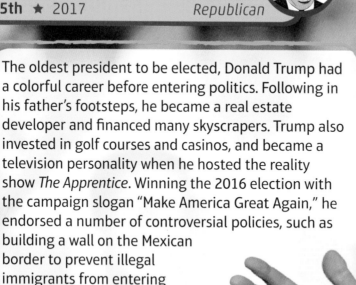

The oldest president to be elected, Donald Trump had a colorful career before entering politics. Following in his father's footsteps, he became a real estate developer and financed many skyscrapers. Trump also invested in golf courses and casinos, and became a television personality when he hosted the reality show *The Apprentice*. Winning the 2016 election with the campaign slogan "Make America Great Again," he endorsed a number of controversial policies, such as building a wall on the Mexican border to prevent illegal immigrants from entering the United States.

REAL ESTATE TYCOON

One of Trump's largest property investments was the Trump International Tower and Hotel in Chicago. Originally intended to be the world's tallest building, it was scaled back after the 2001 attacks, but still soars to 1,389 ft (423.3 m). Completed in 2009, the building cost almost $850,000,000 and has 100 floors and 2.6 million sq ft (241,548 sq m) of floor space.

DATA FILE

BORN: June 14, 1946, New York, New York

INAUGURATED AS PRESIDENT: January 20, 2017, age 70

KEY DATES:

1980 Completes development of the Grand Hyatt Hotel near Grand Central Station, New York City – his first major property deal.

1990 Opens the Taj Mahal casino, in Atlantic City, the largest casino in the world.

2000 Enters the race to seek nomination by the Reform Party for the 2000 presidential elections, but later withdraws his candidacy.

2016 Nominated as the Republican Party's candidate for the presidential race.

For his role in *The Apprentice*, Trump received his own **star** on the **Hollywood Walk of Fame**.

Donald Trump

2 NOTABLE FIRST LADIES

Since Martha Washington in the 18th century, the wives of the US presidents have held a highly visible yet undefined position. Their role has evolved over the centuries, from hosting functions and events in the White House, to using their influence to promote specific causes.

MARTHA WASHINGTON

1789–1797 ★ *President: George Washington*

Brought up on a plantation in Virginia, Martha married George Washington after the death of her first husband Daniel Parke Custis. During the American Revolution, she regularly spent winters at army camps with Washington. After he became president, Martha hosted events for him in the nation's first capitals at New York City and Philadelphia, which were so lavish they were referred to as the "Republican court." Although she was America's *first* first lady, the term was not yet used, and Martha was referred to as "Lady Washington."

Martha is **one of only two women** to **appear** on **US currency**—the other is **Pocahontas.**

DATA FILE

BORN: June 2, 1731, New Kent County, Virginia
DIED: May 22, 1802

MARRIED: January 6, 1759, New Kent County, Virginia

CHILDREN: Daniel, Frances, John, Martha

KEY DATES:

1757   Becomes a widow after the death of her first husband.

1778   Spends the winter at Valley Forge, Pennsylvania, tending to sick soldiers in the Continental Army.

1797   Returns to live at Mount Vernon after the end of George Washington's presidency.

Martha Washington

ABIGAIL ADAMS

1797-1801 ★ *President: John Adams*

Although she had no formal education, Abigail was an avid reader. She championed the cause of educating girls and promoted the rights of married women. She also inspired future first ladies to play an active role in politics. After the American Revolution, Abigail accompanied John Adams on diplomatic postings to France and Great Britain. They were the first presidential couple to live in the White House.

DATA FILE

BORN: November 22, 1744, Weymouth, Massachusetts
DIED: October 28, 1818

MARRIED: October 25, 1764 Weymouth, Massachusetts

CHILDREN: Abigail ("Nabby"), John Quincy, Susanna, Charles, Thomas Boylston

KEY DATES:

1775 Serves on a commission in Massachusetts to test the loyalty of women suspected of working against the Revolution.

1789 Becomes the first second lady when her husband becomes Washington's vice president.

1800 Moves into the White House.

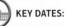

Notable First Ladies

DOLLEY MADISON

1809–1817 ★ *President: James Madison*

A lively and charming hostess, Dolley began the tradition of inaugural balls in Washington, DC. She was the first to decorate the White House, and in 1810, threw a gala to display the remodeled mansion. Dolley is also remembered for the remarkable courage she displayed when the British invaded Washington, DC, during the War of 1812. As British troops advanced to burn the White House, she rescued several national treasures, including a large portrait of George Washington.

DATA FILE

BORN: May 20, 1768, New Garden, North Carolina
DIED: July 12, 1849

MARRIED: September 15, 1794 Harewood, Virginia

CHILDREN: John Payne, William

KEY DATES:

1809 Presides at the first inaugural ball in Washington, DC.

1814 Saves valuables from the White House before it is burned.

1844 Becomes the first private citizen to broadcast a message via Morse Code.

Abigail Adams / Dolley Madison

MARY
LINCOLN

1861–1865 ★ *President: Abraham Lincoln*

Mary was a well-educated, intelligent, and witty woman, but led a troubled life under the pressures of her husband's political success and family tragedy. During the Civil War, she visited patients in the Union army hospitals and supported efforts to raise money to help freed slaves. However, jealous rivals accused her of being a Confederate sympathizer due to her southern roots, and she was also criticised for spending large amounts of money on clothes. The grief she suffered after both the death of her son Willie and her husband's assassination made the last years of her life almost unbearable.

DATA FILE

BORN: December 13, 1818, Lexington, Kentucky

MARRIED: November 4, 1842, Springfield, Illinois

CHILDREN: Robert Todd, Edward Baker, William Wallace, Thomas

KEY DATES:

1861 Spends $26,000 restoring the White House, leading to accusations of extravagance.

1865 Witnesses the assassination of President Lincoln while at Ford's Theatre in Washington, DC.

FRANCES CLEVELAND

1885–1889/1893–1897 ★ *President: Grover Cleveland*

Frances became the *first* first lady to wed in the White House when she married Grover Cleveland, whom she had known since she was a child. The youngest first lady, she was a popular hostess who held receptions on Saturdays so that working women could attend. During her time in Washington, DC, she championed several charities, including those that supported homeless women and families, and others that promoted education for girls.

DATA FILE

BORN: July 21, 1864, Buffalo, New York

MARRIED: June 2, 1886, White House, Washington, DC

CHILDREN: Ruth, Esther, Marion, Richard Folsom, Francis Grover

KEY DATES:

1887 Accompanies President Cleveland on a tour of the southern and western states.

1893 Becomes the first former first lady to return to the White House when Grover Cleveland is reelected for a nonconsecutive second term.

Mary Lincoln/Frances Cleveland

EDITH
WILSON

1915-1921 ★ *President: Woodrow Wilson*

As first lady during World War I, Edith set an example by volunteering with the Red Cross and encouraging rationing in the White House. After the president had a stroke in 1919, she took on a stewardship role, working with his cabinet and reading government papers. By doing this, she hid the poor state of the president's health, allowing him to continue in office.

DATA FILE

BORN: October 15, 1872, Wytheville, Virginia
DIED: December 28, 1961

MARRIED: December 1915, Washington, DC

KEY DATES:

1896   Marries her first husband, businessman Norman Galt, who dies in 1908.

1915   First meets the president, shortly after the death of his first wife Ellen.

1919   Accompanies President Wilson to Europe to attend the peace negotiations at Versailles, at the end of World War I.

LOU
HOOVER

Lou led an active life before becoming first lady. An expert horsewoman and trained geologist, she accompanied Herbert Hoover on his travels as a mining engineer, and later became involved with food relief charities during World War I. As first lady, she lobbied for women's rights and gave radio speeches encouraging Americans as the Great Depression deepened.

DATA FILE

BORN: March 29, 1874, Waterloo, Iowa
DIED: January 7, 1944

MARRIED: February 10, 1899, Monterey, California

CHILDREN: Herbert Clark, Allan Henry

KEY DATES:

1914   Creates and chairs the American Women's War Relief Fund.

1923   Appointed President of the Women's Division of the National Amateur Athletics Association.

When **accompanying** her **husband to China**, Lou **learned Mandarin**.

Edith Wilson / Lou Hoover

ELEANOR ROOSEVELT

1933–1945 ★ *President: Franklin D. Roosevelt*

Eleanor was one of the most active first ladies, and also the longest-serving. A great believer in social reform, she took President Roosevelt on a tour of New York slums early in their courtship. Once he became president, she campaigned on a wide range of social issues. A champion of women's rights, she ensured her husband's New Deal—a social reform program—contained measures to help them. She held press conferences at the White House for female reporters, wrote *My Day*—a daily newspaper column—and gave more than 1,400 speeches during her time as first lady.

Eleanor **helped draft** the **Universal Declaration of Human Rights**.

OFFICIAL VISITS

After she left high school, Eleanor worked for the National Consumers League, visiting slums and reporting on their conditions. As first lady, she continued to visit institutions across the country, including schools, and other government facilities. Her findings encouraged her to promote many new causes.

DATA FILE

BORN: October 11, 1884, New York, New York
DIED: November 7, 1962

MARRIED: March 17, 1905, New York, New York

CHILDREN: Anna Eleanor, James, Elliott, Franklin Delano Jr., John Aspinwall

KEY DATES:

1939 **FEBRUARY** Resigns from the Daughters of the American Revolution (DAR) after they refuse to allow an African American singer to perform at Constitution Hall.

1939 **JUNE** Hosts British monarchs King George VI and Queen Elizabeth when they visit the US.

1946 Leads the UN Commission on Human Rights as chairwoman for six years.

1961 Becomes Chair of the Presidential Commission on the Status of Women.

SPEAKING HER MIND

In this photograph, Eleanor is shown speaking at the annual *Herald Tribune* forum in New York, 1943. Although controversial at the time, her outspokenness made her one of history's most influential first ladies.

Eleanor Roosevelt

JACQUELINE
KENNEDY

1961–1963 ★ *President: John F. Kennedy*

Jacqueline—popularly known as Jackie—brought a sense of style and flair to the office of first lady. A French literature graduate with an interest in the arts, she refurbished the White House and used it to stage opera, jazz, and ballet performances. Jackie accompanied her husband on many trips abroad, making more international tours than any previous first lady. A popular figure, her strength and quiet dignity after the tragic assassination of her husband won her the admiration of millions of people worldwide.

DATA FILE

BORN: July 28, 1929, Southampton, New York
DIED: May 19, 1994

MARRIED: September 12, 1953, Newport, Rhode Island

CHILDREN: Caroline, Patrick, John Fitzgerald Jr.

KEY DATES:

1952　Gets her first job as a reporter for the *Washington Times-Herald*.

1962　Presents a televised tour of the White House.

"LADY BIRD" JOHNSON

1963–1969 ★ *President: Lyndon B. Johnson*

Nicknamed "Lady Bird," Claudia Taylor was born into a well-to-do Texas family. After graduating from college, she bought a small radio station and built it up into a large media business. As first lady, Lady Bird championed civil rights and held "Women Do-er Luncheons" in the White House to promote the accomplishments of leading women in their respective fields. She also supported a program for the beautification of Washington, DC, and helped refurbish decayed public buildings.

DATA FILE

 BORN: December 22, 1912, Karnack, Texas
DIED: July 11, 2007

 MARRIED: November 17, 1934, San Antonio, Texas

 CHILDREN: Lynda Bird, Luci Baines

 KEY DATES:

1965 Becomes honorary chairperson of the Head Start program, which aims to help educate preschool children in poor families.

1982 Founds the Lady Bird Johnson Wildflower Center at the University of Texas.

In **1970**, Lady Bird **published** *A White House Diary* about her experiences as first lady.

Jacqueline Kennedy/"Lady Bird" Johnson

BETTY
FORD

1974–1977 ★ *President: Gerald R. Ford*

Betty studied dance, and worked as a model and a department store fashion coordinator, before becoming first lady. She was a strong champion of women's rights and campaigned to introduce an Equal Rights Amendment to the Constitution. A frank and open first lady, her discussions about her breast cancer surgery inspired other women to talk about the difficult subject. After leaving the White House, she admitted to a long-running struggle with alcoholism.

DATA FILE

BORN: April 8, 1918, Chicago, Illinois
DIED: July 8, 2011

MARRIED: October 15, 1948, Grand Rapids, Michigan

CHILDREN: Michael Gerald, John "Jack" Gardner, Steven Meigs, Susan Elizabeth

KEY DATES:

1975   Becomes the first recipient of the National Woman's Party Alice Paul Award to honor her campaign for the Equal Rights Amendment.

1982   Founds the Betty Ford Center for alcohol and drug dependency, after her own battle with alcoholism.

In **1976**, Betty became the *first* **first lady to appear** in a **television sitcom**.

ROSALYNN CARTER

1977–1981 ★ *President: Jimmy Carter*

A small-town girl, Rosalynn became an active first lady and was the first to attend cabinet meetings. She spoke out on improving mental healthcare, testifying before Congress on the issue. Rosalynn also pushed for the introduction of an Age Discrimination Act to help elderly Americans.

DATA FILE

BORN: August 18, 1927, Plains, Georgia

MARRIED: July 7, 1946, Plains, Georgia

CHILDREN: John William, James Earl III, Donnel Jeffrey, Amy Lynn

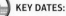

KEY DATES:

1980 Campaigns actively for the passing of the Mental Health Systems Act, which reforms mental health treatment.

1982 Presides as vice chairperson of the Carter Center, a nonprofit organisation founded by her and her husband, which aims to promote health and human rights around the world.

Betty Ford/ Rosalynn Carter

NANCY REAGAN

1981–1989 ★ *President: Ronald Reagan*

Like President Reagan, Nancy was a former Hollywood actor. As first lady, she fought hard for better drug education, and started the "Just Say No" campaign across America. She also supported the Foster Grandparent Program to help children in difficult circumstances. Nancy was fiercely protective of her husband, especially after he suffered an assassination attempt.

DATA FILE

BORN: July 6, 1921, New York, New York
DIED: March 6, 2016

MARRIED: March 4, 1952, San Fernando Valley, California

CHILDREN: Patricia Ann "Patti" and Ronald Prescott

KEY DATES:

1985 Holds a conference in Washington for the first ladies of 17 countries to highlight the problem of drug and alcohol abuse among children.

1988 Becomes the *first* first lady to address the United Nations, asking for tougher laws to prevent the illegal movement of drugs.

Notable First Ladies

BARBARA
BUSH
1989–1993 ★ President: George H.W. Bush

Barbara and George Bush met as teenagers and married during World War II. As first lady, Barbara's warm nature and approachable air gave her a reputation as "America's grandmother." She was active in promoting adult literacy—an interest that stemmed from her son Neil's dyslexia—and organized the Barbara Bush Foundation for Family Literacy. She also supported numerous other causes, including those concerning the homeless and the elderly.

DATA FILE

BORN: June 8, 1925,
Rye, New York

MARRIED: January 6, 1945,
Rye, New York

CHILDREN: George Walker,
Robin, John Ellis, Neil Mallon,
Marvin Pierce, Dorothy Walker

KEY DATES:

1989   Establishes the Barbara Bush
Foundation for Family Literacy.

1994   Publishes her autobiography
Barbara Bush: A Memoir.

Nancy Reagan/ Barbara Bush

HILLARY CLINTON

1993–2001 ★ *President: Bill Clinton*

Born in Chicago, Hillary earned a law degree from Yale University. One of the most politically active first ladies, she was the first to have her own office in the West Wing. As first lady, she pushed for healthcare reforms and also supported measures to help adopted children. In 2000, Hillary became the first presidential spouse to be elected to political office, as a senator for New York State. She then served as Secretary of State for four years.

DATA FILE

BORN: October 26, 1947
Park Ridge, Illinois

MARRIED: October 11, 1975
Fayetteville, Arkansas

CHILDREN: Chelsea

KEY DATES:

1997 Sponsors the Adoption and Safe Family Act to provide extra funds for adopted children and their families.

2009 Appointed Secretary of State.

2016 Becomes the first female presidential nominee of a major political party (the Democrats), losing the election to Republican Donald Trump.

LAURA
BUSH
2001–2009 ★ *President: George W. Bush*

A former schoolteacher, Laura had a strong interest in child literacy. She championed George W. Bush's No Child Left Behind Act to raise the standards of education, particularly in poor areas. Laura also promoted programs such as the New Teacher Project, which aimed to attract professionals from different career backgrounds into teaching. To promote reading at an early age, she created a national initiative called "Ready to Read, Ready to Learn."

DATA FILE

BORN: November 4, 1946, Midland, Texas

MARRIED: November 5, 1977, Midland, Texas

CHILDREN: Barbara, Jenna

KEY DATES:

2002   Establishes The Laura Bush Foundation for America's Libraries.

2004   Helps in the creation of the Preserve America History Teacher of the Year award, a part of her campaign to increase interest in the historical heritage of the United States.

In **2001**, Laura **launched** the **first annual National Book Festival** across the country.

MICHELLE OBAMA

2009–2017 ★ *President: Barack Obama*

A Harvard Law School graduate, Michelle was Vice President of Community Affairs at the University of Chicago before becoming first lady. The first African American first lady, she became a role model for women around the world and championed the right of girls to receive a proper education. In addition to promoting campaigns to reduce child obesity, Michelle also raised awareness of the difficulties faced by military veterans' families, and helped improve access to higher education for poorer students.

Michelle's **Secret Service code name** was **"Renaissance."**

LET'S MOVE

In 2010, Michelle launched "Let's Move," a campaign to reduce childhood obesity levels in the United States, after statistics showed around 40 percent of children were overweight or obese. The campaign aimed to work with communities and educators to promote healthy eating and exercise among the young.

DATA FILE

BORN: January 17, 1964, Chicago, Illinois

MARRIED: October 3, 1992, Chicago, Illinois

CHILDREN: Malia Ann, Natasha "Sasha"

KEY DATES:

2011   Launches "Joining Forces," an initiative to raise awareness of the issues faced by veterans and their families.

2014   Founds "Reach Higher" with the aim of encouraging education beyond high school for children from poorer families.

2015   Launches the "Let Girls Learn" initiative to help girls around the world get access to good schools and further education.

Michelle Obama

3 THE CONSTITUTION AND THE PRESIDENCY

Ever since the founding of the United States, the Constitution has laid out the powers, duties, and responsibilities of the president—the holder of the most important office in the country. Over the years, further constitutional changes have been made to define what the president can do, how the president is elected, and who can vote in the presidential elections.

WHERE HISTORY WAS WRITTEN
Independence Hall in Philadelphia has been the home of many important historical events. Both the Declaration of Independence and the US Constitution were signed in the building.

THE AMERICAN
REVOLUTION

1775–1781

By the 1770s, many settlers in Britain's 13 American colonies had begun to think about establishing their independence. The colonists resented the taxes imposed on them by the British, because they were denied representation in British Parliament. In 1775, war broke out between British soldiers and the colonists. The conflict continued for six years, until in 1781, the last large British force surrendered at Yorktown, bringing the war to a victorious end for the revolutionaries.

DATA FILE

KEY DATES:

1774 The British pass a range of harsh measures against the colonists, known as the Intolerable Acts, in response to the Boston Tea Party.

1775 **APRIL 16** The first battle of the American Revolution takes place at Lexington and Concord, Massachusetts.

1777 **OCTOBER 17** The Continental Army defeats the British at Saratoga.

1781 **OCTOBER 19** After being surrounded at Yorktown, British General Cornwallis surrenders.

THE BOSTON TEA PARTY
In protest of unfair British taxation on imported goods, on December 16, 1773, some rebels, dressed as Native Americans, boarded a British ship in Boston Harbor and threw its cargo of highly taxed tea overboard. This act of defiance is known as the Boston Tea Party.

The Constitution and the Presidency

THE DECLARATION OF
INDEPENDENCE

1776

During the Revolution, the Second Continental Congress met in Philadelphia in June 1776 and decided to begin drafting a Declaration of Independence. Thomas Jefferson authored the first draft of this document, which listed American grievances against the British and the rights the colonists were claiming for themselves. On July 4, 1776, the Declaration officially came into effect, declaring the United States an independent nation.

DATA FILE

KEY FIGURES: Thomas Jefferson, John Adams, Benjamin Franklin

ADOPTED AT: Second Continental Congress, Philadelphia

NUMBER OF STATES SIGNED BY: 13

CURRENT LOCATION: National Archives, Washington, DC

THE COMMITTEE OF FIVE

The Continental Congress appointed a five-member committee to draft the Declaration of Independence, which comprised John Adams, Roger Sherman, Robert R. Livingston, Thomas Jefferson, and Benjamin Franklin (shown here from left to right).

The American Revolution

THE DRAFTING OF THE
CONSTITUTION
1787

In May 1787, delegates from 12 states met at the Constitutional Convention in Philadelphia, Pennsylvania to decide how the new government should operate. There was much debate between those who wanted a strong central government and those who wanted individual states to retain many or most powers. However, after a period of almost four months, 39 delegates signed a final draft. This document established a system of federal governance for the states, and was declared "the supreme law of the land."

DATA FILE

KEY FIGURES: James Madison, Alexander Hamilton

DATE SIGNED: September 17, 1787

NUMBER OF PARTICIPATING STATES: 55 delegates from 12 states. Rhode Island was the only one of the 13 colonies not to send delegates.

DATE RATIFIED BY ALL STATES: May 29, 1790

The Constitution and the Presidency

At **4,400 words**, the **US Constitution** is the **shortest** of all the world's **written national constitutions**.

SIGNING THE CONSTITUTION

In this image, the delegates are pictured gathering to sign the Constitution. After it was signed, the document needed nine states to ratify it to go into effect, which happened on June 21, 1788, when New Hampshire ratified it.

The Drafting of the Constitution

PRESIDENTIAL
POWERS

The powers of the presidency were laid down in the Constitution by the Founding Fathers. They intended for the president to act as the country's chief executive, and gave him or her the ability to sign congressional legislation into law, and to veto (reject) any legislation he or she does not approve of. The president also has an important international role as a figurehead for the country, and can make treaties with foreign states. Other presidential powers include the ability to appoint ambassadors and Supreme Court justices, and to grant pardons. Although not explicitly mentioned in the Constitution, the president may also issue executive orders that have the force of law.

FIRST INAUGURATION
George Washington began the tradition of an inaugural address given by the president. He is shown here taking the oath of office at his inauguration at Federal Hall, New York City, on April 30, 1789.

COMMANDER-IN-CHIEF

The Constitution appoints the president as commander-in-chief of the armed forces, but also gives Congress the sole power to declare war. Although Congress has granted some presidents additional powers during wartime, such as President Roosevelt during World War II, the original overlapping powers have often caused confusion. In 1973, Congress passed the War Powers Resolution to address this, which limited the president's ability to send troops overseas without congressional approval.

President **Franklin D. Roosevelt** issued the **most executive orders**—a total of **3,522**.

DATA FILE

REQUIREMENTS: Must be a natural-born citizen, aged 35 or older, and have been a resident in the United States for 14 years.

TIME IN OFFICE: Term of four years, maximum of two terms (since 1951)

ORDER OF SUCCESSION: Should the president die or leave office unexpectedly, he or she is succeeded first by the vice president, and then in the following order by the speaker of the House of Representatives, president of the Senate, and Secretary of State.

SALARY: $400,000 (since 2001)

PRESIDENTIAL
ELECTIONS

The earliest presidential elections in the United States were simple affairs, with small groups of electors voting at local gatherings. However, the electorate steadily increased to include all men (from 1870) and women (from 1920), and today there are around 215 million potential voters. Parties often spend vast sums of money to campaign for their candidates on many different media platforms. The 2012 campaign cost the two main parties around $2.6 billion in total. Upon winning, the successful candidate does not take office immediately; there is a two-month transition period during which the outgoing president still holds office.

DATA FILE

HELD: Every four years
ELECTION DAY: First tuesday in November
INAUGURATION DAY: March 4 until 1933; January 20 since 1937

PRESIDENTIAL OATH:
"I do solemnly swear (or affirm) that I will faithfully execute the Office of President of the United States, and will to the best of my ability, preserve, protect and defend the Constitution of the United States."

REELECTION CAMPAIGN
Presidential candidates often hold big events to attract supporters. Pictured here, President George H. W. Bush and his wife campaign for reelection in 1992.

THE ELECTORAL SYSTEM

Since the presidential elections of 1796, candidates have been chosen by their political party. From 1901, this has been done through primaries and caucuses—events where party members vote for whom they would like to represent them. Candidates from each party then compete against each other. However, the popular vote does not directly decide the winner. In most states, the candidate who wins the vote gets to appoint their supporters as that state's electors. The appointed electors from all the states form an Electoral College, and they then vote for the future president.

DATA FILE

MAIN PRESIDENTIAL PARTIES:
Republican and Democrat

DATE OF ELECTORAL COLLEGE VOTE COUNT:
January 6

ORIGINAL SIZE OF ELECTORAL COLLEGE (1789): 69 electors
CURRENT SIZE OF ELECTORAL COLLEGE (1789): 538 electors

☞ Political Parties **pp200–01**

Presidential Elections

THE PRESIDENT AND CONGRESS

Established in 1787, Congress comprises two houses: the Senate and the House of Representatives. Through a system of checks, put in place by the Constitution, the powers of Congress and the president are balanced. The president can veto legislation proposed by Congress, while presidential appointments and treaties must be approved by the Senate. Congress also has to approve the federal budget, which is submitted by the president. When Congress is controlled by a party different from that of the president, initiatives proposed by one are often blocked by the other—leading to a state known as "gridlock."

DATA FILE

CONSTITUTIONAL PROVISION:
"Every Bill which shall have passed the House of Representatives and the Senate, shall, before it become a Law, be presented to the President of the United States; If he approve he shall sign it, but if not he shall return it, with his Objections to that House in which it shall have originated."

DATE OF FIRST PRESIDENTIAL VETO: April 5, 1792 (by George Washington)
NUMBER OF PRESIDENTIAL VETOES: 2,572 (to August 2016)

PRESIDENTS EXERCISING LARGEST NUMBER OF VETOES:
Franklin D. Roosevelt: 635
Grover Cleveland: 414
Harry S. Truman: 250

By tradition, the State of the Union Address is one of the few occasions when the president addresses Congress. Here, President Obama speaks at a joint session of Congress on January 25, 2011.

PRESIDENTIAL VETO

Although presidents have the power to veto bills that they disapprove of, a presidential veto can be overridden by a two-thirds vote in both the Senate and the House of Representatives. In 1996, an act passed by Congress also granted presidents the power of line-item veto (to veto specific parts of a bill). However, the Supreme Court later ruled this unconstitutional and Bill Clinton remains the only president to have exercised this power.

THE BILL OF
RIGHTS

After the Constitution was signed, many in Congress felt it did not sufficiently protect the personal liberties of citizens. This group—called the Anti-Federalists—lobbied for amendments to guarantee individual rights and freedoms. Responding to these calls, James Madison proposed a list of changes, and in 1791, ten amendments were introduced to the Constitution. Collectively known as the Bill of Rights, these cover a range of entitlements, from freedom of speech to the right to trial by jury.

DATA FILE

KEY PROVISIONS:
First Amendment: Right to freedom of speech and religion.
Second Amendment: Right to bear arms.
Fifth Amendment: Right to refuse to give evidence against oneself in court.
Sixth Amendment: Right to trial by jury.
Tenth Amendment: All powers not given by the Constitution to the federal government to remain with the states.

FIRST INTRODUCTION:
July 21, 1789

CONGRESSIONAL APPROVAL:
September 25, 1789

DATE OF RATIFICATION (10 ARTICLES): December 15, 1791

The Constitution and the Presidency

THE NATIONAL ARCHIVES

Altogether, 14 handwritten copies of the Bill of Rights were made—one for the federal government and one for each of the 13 states. Today, the American government's copy is housed in the National Archives in Washington, DC, where visitors can view the original document on display.

The Bill of Rights

The Bill of Rights

THE CIVIL WAR

1861–1865

Only 80 years after the American Revolution, a bitter conflict threatened to destroy the Union. Fearing slavery might be abolished, in 1861, seven southern states left the Union and established the Confederate States of America. They later attacked Fort Sumter in Charleston Harbor, South Carolina, beginning the Civil War and causing four more states to leave the Union and join their cause. Fighting escalated quickly, but despite the efforts of talented generals such as Robert E. Lee, the Confederacy remained a weaker force. A Union victory at Gettysburg in 1863 left the south on the defensive, and its last large force surrendered in April 1865. By the end of the war, around 620,000 soldiers had lost their lives.

DATA FILE

UNION STATES: 20
CONFEDERATE STATES: 11

KEY DATES:

1861 APRIL Confederate troops attack Fort Sumter, South Carolina.

1861 JULY The first Battle of Bull Run, Virginia, is fought.

1862 DECEMBER Confederate troops win a decisive victory at the Battle of Fredericksburg, Virginia.

1863 JULY The Union wins the bloodiest battle of the Civil War at Gettysburg, Pennsylvania.

1865 APRIL General Robert E. Lee surrenders to General Ulysses S. Grant at Appomattox Court House, Virginia.

THE CONFEDERATE STATES

Formed in February 1861, the Confederate States of America included the 11 southern states that had left the Union. Its first (and only) president was Jefferson Davis, who had previously been a senator from Mississippi as well as Secretary of War. This painting depicts his inauguration in Montgomery, Alabama, in February 1861.

THE SIEGE OF VICKSBURG
Union troops attacked the Confederate defensive lines during the Siege of Vicksburg, Mississippi, in 1863. The siege ended with the capture of the last Confederate stronghold on the Mississippi River.

13TH AMENDMENT
ABOLITION OF SLAVERY

1865

The issue of whether or not to allow slavery had plagued the United States since its foundation, and ultimately led to the Civil War. President Lincoln's Emancipation Proclamation of 1863 freed many slaves, but it did not legally abolish slavery. As the Civil War drew to a close, the nation debated the need for a new constitutional amendment to outlaw this practice. Although there was fierce opposition, the 13th Amendment was successfully passed in January 1865.

14TH AMENDMENT

The abolition of slavery did not stop discrimination against former slaves. Congress passed a Civil Rights Act in 1866, but this did not sufficiently protect the legal rights of African Americans. Finally, the 14th Amendment was passed to guarantee all American citizens equal protection under the law. This came into effect in 1868.

The Constitution and the Presidency

Around **4 million slaves** were **freed** by the **passing** of the **13th Amendment**.

CELEBRATING LIBERTY

Former slaves celebrate the passing of the 13th Amendment, displaying copies of newspapers that proclaimed the news of their freedom.

Abolition of Slavery

15TH AMENDMENT
VOTING RIGHTS
1870

In 1870, the Republicans helped pass the 15th Amendment, guaranteeing the right to vote to all men, regardless of their race or color. This law complemented the 13th and 14th amendments, which had abolished slavery and extended citizenship to African Americans. However, the new amendment did not stop states from imposing conditions on voters, such as taxes or literacy tests. This prevented many African Americans from exercising their right to vote, especially in the south.

The state of **Tennessee did not ratify** the 15th amendment **until 1997**.

DATA FILE

MAIN PROVISION: "The right of citizens of the United States to vote shall not be denied or abridged by the United States or by any State on account of race, color, or previous condition of servitude."

FIRST INTRODUCTION:
January 30, 1869

DATE OF RATIFICATION:
February 3, 1870

Voting Rights

18TH AMENDMENT
PROHIBITION
1919

In the late 19th century, concern that drinking alcohol caused violence led to calls for it to be banned. Many states passed legislation outlawing alcohol and the Anti-Saloon League led a campaign for an amendment to ban it nationally. The passing of the 18th Amendment and the Volstead Act, which specified the types of alcohol that were banned, began an era known as "Prohibition." However, a lack of money to pay for inspectors to enforce this ban led to the growth of "speakeasies"—illegal bars where alcohol could still be bought. Crime also rose, as gangsters such as Al Capone in Chicago took over the illegal alcohol trade.

DATA FILE

MAIN PROVISION: "After one year from the ratification of this article the manufacture, sale, or transportation of intoxicating liquors within, the importation thereof into, or the exportation thereof from the United States and all territory subject to the jurisdiction thereof for beverage purposes is hereby prohibited."

FIRST INTRODUCTION:
August 1, 1917

CONGRESSIONAL APPROVAL:
December 18, 1917

DATE OF RATIFICATION:
January 16, 1919

ILLEGAL TRADE
In New York City, there were tens of thousands of speakeasies during the Prohibition era. In this image, police watch as government agents pour barrels of illegal alcohol down the sewers.

21ST AMENDMENT

Rising crime and the loss of government income from alcohol taxes led to the 18th Amendment being repealed. The 21st Amendment, ratified in December 1933, made the sale of alcohol legal again, much to the delight of many Americans.

FAREWELL 18TH AMENDMENT

19TH AMENDMENT
WOMEN'S SUFFRAGE

1920

Although during the 19th century voting rights had been extended to many men, American women were still not allowed to vote. The struggle to obtain this right—known as suffrage—began in 1848 when a women's rights convention in Seneca Falls, New York, listed it as a fundamental right in their "Declaration of Sentiments." Women's groups began to lobby for a constitutional amendment, but it took many years to get it passed. By this time, many women had been granted voting rights by their states, but it was only in the federal elections on November 2, 1920, that all American women could vote.

CELEBRATING VICTORY

A crowd cheers women's suffrage campaigner Alice Paul as she unfurls a banner to celebrate the ratification of the 19th Amendment by Tennessee. This meant that the amendment had been ratified by enough states to come into effect.

The Constitution and the Presidency

DATA FILE

MAIN PROVISION: "The right of citizens of the United States to vote shall not be denied or abridged by the United States or by any State on account of sex."

FIRST INTRODUCTION: January 1878

CONGRESSIONAL APPROVAL: June 4, 1919

DATE OF RATIFICATION: August 18, 1920

VOTES FOR WOMEN

The National Woman Suffrage Association (NWSA) was founded in May 1869 by Susan B. Anthony and Elizabeth Cady Stanton. More radical than other women's rights groups, it organized protests and argued strongly for a new constitutional amendment to guarantee voting rights for women. Some of its members even tried to register to vote.

22ND AMENDMENT
TWO-TERM LIMIT
1951

The Constitution set no limit on the number of terms a president could serve, but, following the example of George Washington, it had become customary to serve only two terms at most. When Franklin D. Roosevelt won election to a fourth term in 1944, it sparked a heated debate in Congress. The Democrats argued that the people's right to choose a president should not be restricted. The Republican argument, that the presidency should not be dominated by one person, won out and led to the 22nd Amendment, which barred presidents from serving for more than two terms.

DATA FILE

MAIN PROVISION: "No person shall be elected to the office of the President more than twice, and no person who has held the office of President, or acted as President, for more than two years of a term to which some other person was elected President shall be elected to the office of the President more than once."

CONGRESSIONAL APPROVAL: March 24, 1947

DATE OF RATIFICATION: February 27, 1951

The Constitution and the Presidency

ROOSEVELT FOR VICTORY
A crowd in Chicago carry placards calling for the reelection of Franklin D. Roosevelt during the 1944 election campaign, which ended with him winning an unprecedented fourth term in office.

26TH AMENDMENT
RIGHT TO VOTE AT 18
1971

The Constitution had set the voting age at 21. However, resentment built up during the Vietnam War when young Americans could be called up to serve in the war at 18, but were still not allowed to vote. After the Supreme Court ruled in 1970 that 18–20-year-olds should be allowed to vote in state elections, Congress moved to pass a constitutional amendment to allow them to do so in federal elections. The amendment was ratified just 107 days after its congressional approval, faster than any other amendment to the Constitution.

DATA FILE

MAIN PROVISION: "The right of citizens of the United States, who are eighteen years of age or older, to vote shall not be denied or abridged by the United States or by any State on account of age."

FIRST INTRODUCTION: March 10, 1971

CONGRESSIONAL APPROVAL: March 23, 1971

DATE OF RATIFICATION: July 1, 1971

REGISTERING TO VOTE
Students at Westchester High School, California, line up to register to vote in 1971. The slogan "Old enough to fight, old enough to vote" had been key in winning them this right.

Two-term Limit

4 PRESIDENTIAL PLACES AND VEHICLES

As the demands of the office have become more complex, presidents have been granted a variety of facilities to assist them in performing their job, including specialized offices, such as the West Wing. Presidents have also used residences and retreats outside Washington, DC, and a series of official aircraft and land vehicles to transport them securely.

WELCOMING THE PRESIDENT
President Obama's official car and a convoy of security wait to greet him as he arrives in Hanover, Germany, on Air Force One.

THE WHITE HOUSE

The White House is the official residence of the president and houses his or her personal and executive offices. Work on the building began in 1792, during Washington's presidency, but was completed only in 1800, when John and Abigail Adams became the first presidential couple to live in the White House. Its first major renovation happened after the War of 1812, and in 1902, Theodore Roosevelt spent more than $500,000 on refurbishments. Over the years, many presidents and first ladies have redecorated the interior of the White House according to their tastes.

The southern façade

The **White House** has **132 rooms**, **35 bathrooms**, eight staircases, and three elevators.

THE BURNING OF WASHINGTON, DC

In August 1814, during the War of 1812, British troops occupied Washington, DC, and set fire to the White House, completely destroying its interior. It took three years to complete the repairs before James and Dolley Madison could move back in.

DATA FILE

YEAR COMPLETED: 1800

ARCHITECT: James Hoban

LOCATION: 1600 Pennsylvania Avenue NW, Washington, DC

COST TO BUILD: $232,000

The White House

THE OVAL OFFICE

The Oval Office is the formal office of the president where he or she holds meetings with heads of state, diplomats, and other dignitaries. It was originally built in 1909 for President Taft and was located at the center of the West Wing. In 1934, Franklin D. Roosevelt moved the office to the southeast corner of the West Wing, overlooking the Rose Garden. By tradition, this oval-shaped room is redecorated by the current president—only the presidential seal on the ceiling and the two flags behind the desk remain the same.

DATA FILE

YEAR COMPLETED: 1934

ARCHITECT: Nathan C. Wyeth

LOCATION: White House, 1600 Pennsylvania Avenue NW, Washington, DC

Each **departing president** leaves a **note** in the Oval Office for his or her **successor**, offering some **advice**.

PRESIDENTIAL MEETING
Shortly after winning the 2008 election, Barack Obama meets with sitting president George W. Bush in the Oval Office. Presidents often confer with their predecessors on the important issues of the day.

The Oval Office

THE WEST WING

The West Wing is the official presidential workplace. It contains a variety of offices, such as the Oval Office, the Cabinet Office—where the president meets with members of the Cabinet—and the Situation Room, which is used as a center for emergency operations. The construction of the West Wing began after Theodore Roosevelt realized the executive mansion did not offer enough room to carry out all presidential duties. The building has been enlarged several times and has become the hub of activity at the White House.

Outside view

PRESIDENTIAL ADVISORS
President Lyndon B. Johnson meets with the National Security Council and other officials on October 31, 1968.

EISENHOWER EXECUTIVE
OFFICE BUILDING

Located opposite the West Wing, the Eisenhower Executive Office Building houses the offices of the vice president and the National Security Council. Originally built for the State, War, and Navy Departments, it took 17 years to be completed. It was gradually acquired by the White House between 1939 and 1949. Decorated with elaborate columns, the building has a distinctive architectural style, and was described by author Mark Twain as "the ugliest building in America."

DATA FILE

YEAR COMPLETED: 1888

ARCHITECT: Alfred B. Mullett

LOCATION: 1650 Pennsylvania Avenue NW, Washington, DC

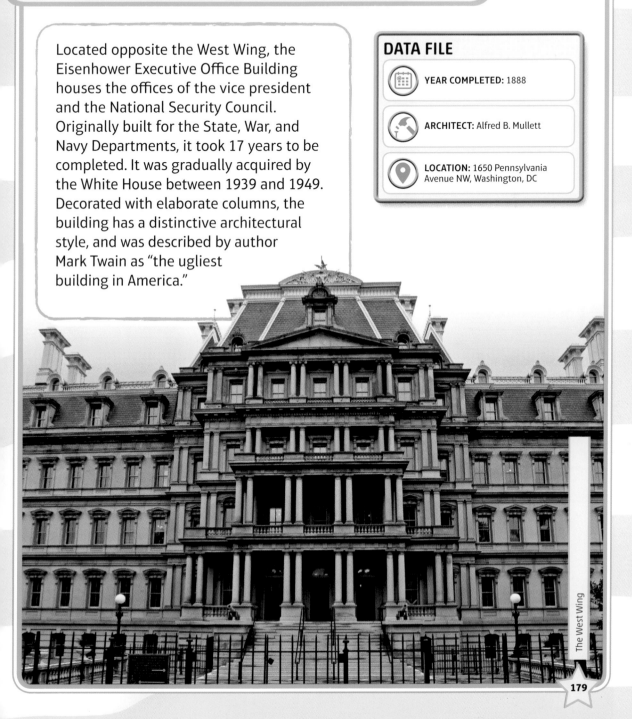

The West Wing

BLAIR HOUSE

The presidential guest house for visiting heads of state, Blair House is located across the street from the White House. Originally built in 1824, it was acquired in 1942 by President Franklin D. Roosevelt. The building is made up of four connected townhouses, with more than 120 rooms and a staff of 18 full-time employees. Notable guests who have stayed at Blair House include British Prime Minister Margaret Thatcher, French President Charles de Gaulle, and Russian President Vladimir Putin. In addition to hosting foreign dignitaries, the building is also used as a venue for events and becomes a residence for presidents-elect in the days prior to their inauguration.

Whenever **foreign leaders** stay in Blair House, the **flag of their country** flies outside the building.

THE TRUMAN WHITE HOUSE

In 1948, during the presidency of Harry S. Truman, it was found that the White House needed extensive renovations. The president and his family moved into Blair House and lived there for the next four years. During this time, it was popularly known as the "Truman White House."

Blair House

CAMP DAVID

Set in the mountains of Maryland, Camp David provides a weekend home for presidents. It was originally built as a camp for federal employees, but in 1942, Franklin D. Roosevelt had it remodeled as a presidential retreat, and called it "Shangri-La." Camp David is also used by presidents to host foreign heads of state. In 1978, President Carter used it as the venue for the historic peace talks between the Egyptian President Anwar Sadat and the Israeli Prime Minister Menachem Begin.

DATA FILE

YEAR COMPLETED: 1938

CONSTRUCTED BY: Works Progress Administration

LOCATION: Catoctin Mountain Park, Frederick County, Maryland

President **Eisenhower** named Camp David **after** both **his father** and **his grandson**.

NUMBER ONE
OBSERVATORY CIRCLE

Acquired by the federal government in 1974, Number One Observatory Circle is the official residence of the vice president and his or her family. The mansion was built in 1893, and previously housed senior naval officers. Walter Mondale became the first vice president to move into the house in 1977, and since then the building has undergone extensive remodeling. Many vice presidents have even added additional features to the residence, including a swimming pool.

DATA FILE

YEAR COMPLETED: 1893

ARCHITECT: Leon E. Dessez

LOCATION: 3450 Massachusetts Avenue NW, Washington, DC

Camp David

MOUNT VERNON

Mount Vernon was the private residence of George and Martha Washington. The Virginia estate belonged to George's father, Augustine, who started the construction of a small house there. When George acquired the estate in 1754, he ordered the building of a grander house in the classical Palladian style, modeled on villas in Italy. In the years following his retirement, Washington hosted hundreds of guests at Mount Vernon. The house later fell into disrepair until it was restored by the Mount Vernon Ladies Association in 1858. It is now a National Historic Landmark.

Inside view, 1925

DATA FILE

YEAR COMPLETED: 1758

ARCHITECT: Unknown

LOCATION: Fairfax County, Virginia

MONTICELLO

Inside view—hallway

Monticello was the private home of Thomas Jefferson. A man of many talents, Jefferson designed the house himself and modeled it on the neoclassical style of the villas he saw while serving as ambassador to France. The 33-room house was surrounded by a vast botanic garden, which was used by Jefferson to breed plants and grow many varieties of vegetables. After his death in 1826, Jefferson was buried at Monticello. The property was bought by the Thomas Jefferson Foundation in 1923 and opened to the public.

Monticello was **seized by the Confederacy** during the Civil War.

DATA FILE

CONSTRUCTION BEGAN: 1769
YEAR COMPLETED: 1809

DESIGNED BY: Thomas Jefferson

LOCATION: Albemarle County, Virginia

Mount Vernon

MOUNT
RUSHMORE

Created as a tribute to the American presidency, Mount Rushmore features the faces of George Washington, Thomas Jefferson, Theodore Roosevelt, and Abraham Lincoln—all carved into a giant granite cliff. South Dakota's state historian, Doane Robinson, commissioned the work in 1923 by Gutzon Borglum, a Danish immigrant and expert sculptor, famous for large-scale stonework. Using jackhammers, chisels, and dynamite, Borglum carved the four faces for 18 years, leaving their completion to his son Lincoln when he passed away. The finished statues stand as a symbol of democracy and are visited by many people from around the world.

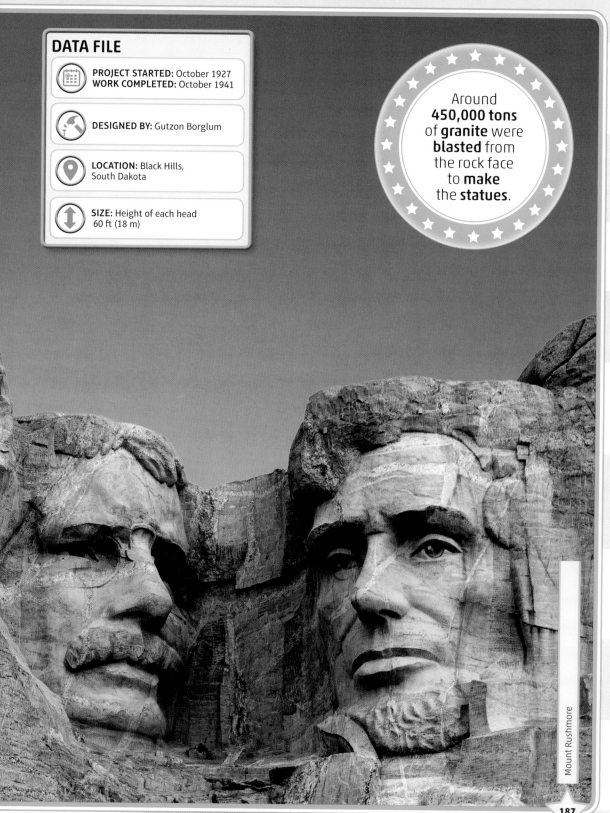

DATA FILE

📅 **PROJECT STARTED:** October 1927
WORK COMPLETED: October 1941

🔨 **DESIGNED BY:** Gutzon Borglum

📍 **LOCATION:** Black Hills, South Dakota

↕ **SIZE:** Height of each head 60 ft (18 m)

Around **450,000 tons** of **granite** were **blasted** from the rock face to **make** the **statues**.

Mount Rushmore

AIR FORCE ONE

Air Force One is the president's official plane, which is often used for visits overseas. The first Air Force One was a Boeing 707, which was delivered to President Kennedy in 1962. This was later upgraded to a Boeing 747 in 1990. Currently, there are two identical aircraft that serve as presidential planes, each including a conference room, a media room, an operating room, 85 telephones, and a presidential bedroom suite. The call sign "Air Force One" is also used to refer to any plane the president is traveling in.

DATA FILE

YEAR FIRST USED: 1962

MADE BY: Boeing

HOME BASE: Joint Base Andrews, Prince George's County, Maryland

LENGTH: 250 ft (76 m)

Inside view

Each official plane stands as tall as a **six-story building**.

CADILLAC ONE

In 1939, Franklin D. Roosevelt became the first president to own a specially built state car, called "Sunshine One." The current car, officially designated "Cadillac One," was given to President Obama in 2009. In the wake of President Kennedy's assassination, presidential cars became increasingly well protected, and Cadillac One is designed with five layers of armor. Nicknamed "The Beast" for its sheer size, the car can withstand attacks by chemical weapons, and has secure communication facilities. Cadillac One even has its own personal plane—a C-17 Globemaster—to airlift it to the place the president is visiting.

DATA FILE

YEAR FIRST USED: 2009 (current model)

MADE BY: General Motors

LENGTH: 18 ft (5.5 m)

The Beast **weighs** more than **15,000 pounds** (6,800 kilograms).

GROUND FORCE ONE

Until 2011, whenever presidents needed to be transported by bus, one was acquired and specially customized. Since this was expensive and did not meet increasing security requirements, the Secret Service commissioned two special armored buses as permanent presidential vehicles. Nicknamed "Ground Force One," these buses have armored exteriors and specially reinforced glass, as well as housing secure communication equipment and an extra supply of the president's blood in case he or she is injured. The buses are even big enough to conduct meetings inside.

DATA FILE

YEAR FIRST USED: 2012

MADE BY: Prevost Cars and Hempthill Brothers Coach Company

LOCATION: Washington, DC

LENGTH: 45 ft (14 m)

The two **Ground Force One** buses cost **$1.1 million** each.

MARINE FORCE ONE

Dwight D. Eisenhower was the first president to travel by helicopter, in 1957, and since then presidents have often used them to get around safely. Marine Force One normally refers to the helicopter carrying the US president, a fleet of which is operated by a squadron of the Marines known as the "Nighthawks." The current models, the VH-60N White Hawk and VH-3D Sea King, carry antimissile systems and allow secure communications. When carrying the president, Marine Force One flies with several other decoy helicopters at its side.

DATA FILE

YEAR FIRST USED: 1957

MADE BY: Sikorsky Aircraft Corporation

LOCATION: Marine Corps Air Facility Quantico, Virginia

LENGTH: 65 ft (20 m)

Ground Force One

5
REFERENCE

Find out some amazing behind-the-scenes facts about the nation's presidents—where they came from, their vice presidents, and some of their shocking election victories. Discover also a collection of fun trivia about presidents' hobbies and some of their most famous pets.

GRAND TRIBUTE

Built to honor the 16th president of the United States, Abraham Lincoln, the Lincoln Memorial in Washington, DC, is one of several monuments designed to commemorate US presidents. Many presidents also have a presidential library named after them, which often contains records and historical artifacts relating to their time in office.

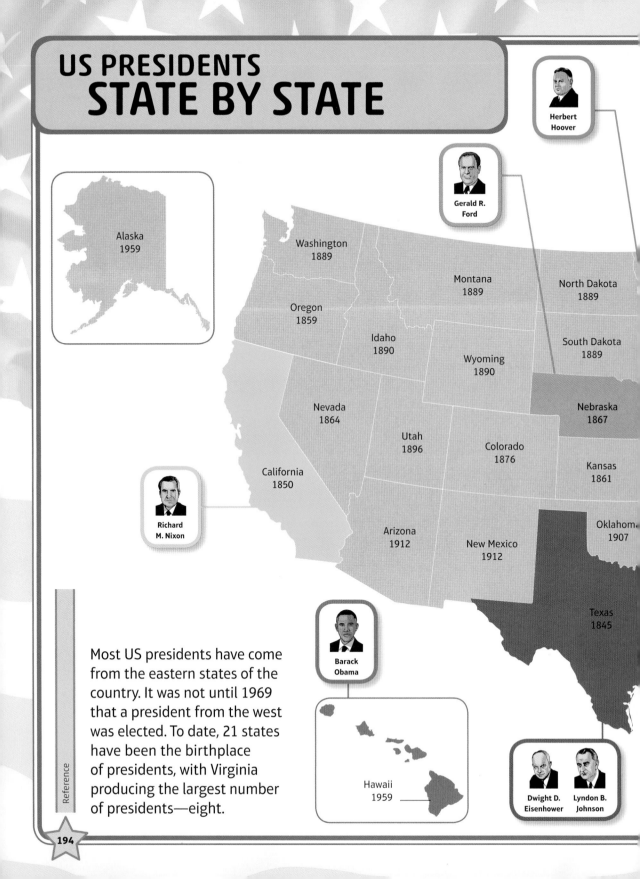

Herbert Hoover

Gerald R. Ford

Alaska
1959

Washington
1889

Montana
1889

North Dakota
1889

Oregon
1859

Idaho
1890

Wyoming
1890

South Dakota
1889

Nevada
1864

Utah
1896

Colorado
1876

Nebraska
1867

California
1850

Richard
M. Nixon

Kansas
1861

Arizona
1912

New Mexico
1912

Oklahoma
1907

Texas
1845

Barack
Obama

Most US presidents have come from the eastern states of the country. It was not until 1969 that a president from the west was elected. To date, 21 states have been the birthplace of presidents, with Virginia producing the largest number of presidents—eight.

Hawaii
1959

Dwight D.
Eisenhower

Lyndon B.
Johnson

Reference

Ulysses S. Grant · Rutherford B. Hayes · James A. Garfield · Benjamin Harrison · William McKinley · William H. Taft · Warren G. Harding

Franklin Pierce

The states highlighted on this map show the birthplace of each US president. Dates indicate when each state joined the Union.

Harry S. Truman

Abraham Lincoln

Grover Cleveland

Chester A. Arthur · Calvin Coolidge

John Adams · John Quincy Adams · John F. Kennedy · George H. W. Bush

Minnesota 1858

Vermont 1791

Maine 1820

New Hampshire 1789

Wisconsin 1848

Michigan 1837

New York 1788

Massachusetts 1788

Rhode Island 1790

George W. Bush

Iowa 1846

Indiana 1816

Ohio 1803

Pennsylvania 1787

Connecticut 1788

Illinois 1818

New Jersey 1787

Martin Van Buren · Millard Fillmore · Theodore Roosevelt

Missouri 1821

Kentucky 1792

Virginia 1788

Delaware 1787

Franklin D. Roosevelt · Donald Trump

Tennessee 1796

Maryland 1788

James Buchanan

Arkansas 1836

South Carolina 1788

West Virginia 1863

Mississippi 1817

Georgia 1788

North Carolina 1789

Andrew Jackson

James K. Polk · Andrew Johnson

Louisiana 1812

Alabama 1819

Florida 1845

George Washington · Thomas Jefferson · James Madison · James Monroe · William H. Harrison

Ronald Reagan

Bill Clinton

Jimmy Carter

John Tyler · Zachary Taylor · Woodrow Wilson

EXTRAORDINARY ELECTIONS

Presidential elections are always a time of great political excitement. Some elections, however, have provoked more interest than others, either because they have marked a change in the nation's political direction, or because they have been extremely close or controversial.

1860

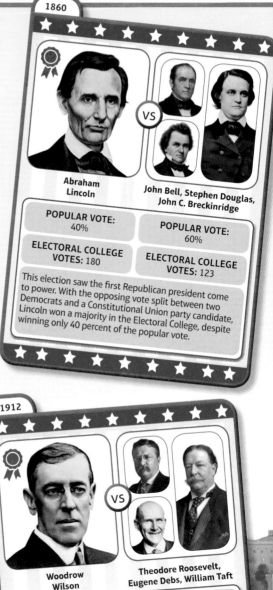

Abraham Lincoln

John Bell, Stephen Douglas, John C. Breckinridge

POPULAR VOTE: 40%	POPULAR VOTE: 60%
ELECTORAL COLLEGE VOTES: 180	ELECTORAL COLLEGE VOTES: 123

This election saw the first Republican president come to power. With the opposing vote split between two Democrats and a Constitutional Union party candidate, Lincoln won a majority in the Electoral College, despite winning only 40 percent of the popular vote.

1876

Samuel J. Tilden

Rutherford B. Hayes

POPULAR VOTE: 51%	POPULAR VOTE: 48%
ELECTORAL COLLEGE VOTES: 184	ELECTORAL COLLEGE VOTES: 185

In this incredibly close election, there were three states where the vote count was disputed and Congress had to set up a 15-person electoral commission to rule on the matter. Eight members of this commission awarded the disputed states to Hayes, and he won the election by a single Electoral College vote.

1912

Woodrow Wilson

Theodore Roosevelt, Eugene Debs, William Taft

POPULAR VOTE: 42%	POPULAR VOTE: 56%
ELECTORAL COLLEGE VOTES: 435	ELECTORAL COLLEGE VOTES: 96

In this rare four-way contest, former president Theodore Roosevelt chose to stand for the Progressive Party. This split the Republican vote and allowed Wilson, with his promise of greater rights for workers, to win an overwhelming majority in the Electoral College.

1932

Franklin D. Roosevelt VS **Herbert Hoover**

POPULAR VOTE: 57%	POPULAR VOTE: 40%
ELECTORAL COLLEGE VOTES: 472	ELECTORAL COLLEGE VOTES: 59

During the Great Depression, Franklin D. Roosevelt's promise of a "New Deal" struck a chord with the voters. He amassed an overwhelming Electoral College majority, winning in 42 states. His subsequent four terms in office began a new wave of Democrat dominance.

1948

Thomas E. Dewey Strom Thurmond VS **Harry S. Truman**

POPULAR VOTE: 45%	POPULAR VOTE: 50%
ELECTORAL COLLEGE VOTES: 189	ELECTORAL COLLEGE VOTES: 303

Harry Truman's chances of winning the presidential election of 1948 looked bleak against his Republican rival Thomas Dewey and Strom Thurmond's Dixiecrats, who undermined his chances in the south. Newspaper headlines on election night declared Dewey the victor, but when results came through, it became clear that Truman had won an astonishing victory.

1980

Ronald Reagan VS **Jimmy Carter**

POPULAR VOTE: 51%	POPULAR VOTE: 48%
ELECTORAL COLLEGE VOTES: 489	ELECTORAL COLLEGE VOTES: 49

Although he was a Republican candidate, Reagan's promise to cut taxes and curb inflation appealed to "Reagan Democrats"—working-class voters who would have traditionally voted for a Democrat. Reagan won by a huge margin, defeating both President Carter, a Democrat, and the third-party candidate John B. Anderson.

2000

Al Gore VS **George W. Bush**

POPULAR VOTE: 48.5%	POPULAR VOTE: 48%
ELECTORAL COLLEGE VOTES: 266	ELECTORAL COLLEGE VOTES: 271

A hard-fought campaign between Al Gore and George W. Bush ended in one of the most controversial electoral counts in American history. The result hung on disputed ballots from the state of Florida. Gore's supporters wanted these recounted by hand, but the Supreme Court ruled against this. Bush was awarded Florida's electoral votes and won a majority of just five Electoral College votes.

VICE PRESIDENTS

Although recent holders of the office have taken on a more active role, the vice president has few formal powers. However, as president of the Senate, he or she casts a deciding vote in the event of a tie and also succeeds the president if he or she resigns or dies.

John Adams
VP for George Washington

1789   179

Richard M. Johnson
VP for Martin Van Buren

Daniel D. Tompkins
VP for James Monroe

John C. Calhoun
VP for John Quincy Adams

John C. Calhoun
VP for Andrew Jackson

Martin Van Buren
VP for Andrew Jackson

1825   1829   1832   1833   1837

Hannibal Hamlin
VP for Abraham Lincoln

Andrew Johnson
VP for Abraham Lincoln

Henry Wilson
VP for Ulysses S. Grant

Chester A. Arthur
VP for James A. Garfield

Schuyler Colfax
VP for Ulysses S. Grant

William A. Wheeler
VP for Rutherford B. Hayes

1865   1865 (APRIL)   1869   1873   1875   1877   1881

1881 (SEPTEMBER)

CHARLES W. FAIRBANKS
Fairbanks was a typical vice president of the era who did not attend cabinet meetings and spent much of his time presiding over the Senate.

Calvin Coolidge
VP for Warren G. Harding

Charles W. Fairbanks
VP for Theodore Roosevelt

Thomas R. Marshall
VP for Woodrow Wilson

1905   1909   1912   1913   1921   1923

James S. Sherman
VP for William H. Taft

Lyndon B. Johnson
VP for John F. Kennedy

Alben W. Barkley
VP for Harry S. Truman

Richard M. Nixon
VP for Dwight D. Eisenhower

1949   1953   1961   1963   1965

ALBERT GORE, JR.
Gore worked on several issues, including digital technology, the environment, and cutting wasteful bureaucracy.

RICHARD CHENEY
Cheney was heavily involved in government, particularly in overseeing military and national security plans.

J. Danforth Quayle
VP for George H. W. Bush

Albert Gore, Jr.
VP for Bill Clinton

Richard Cheney
VP for George W. Bush

1989   1993   2001

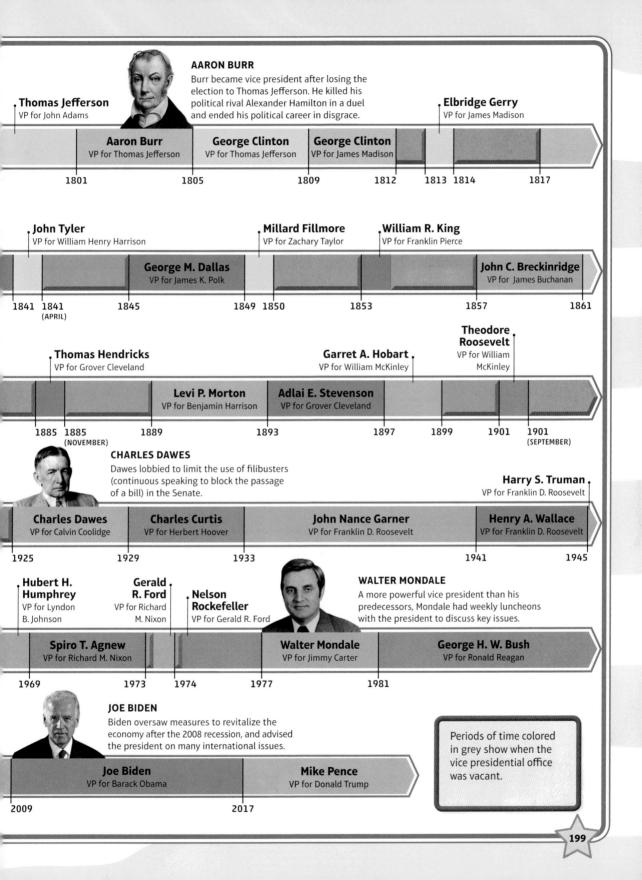

AARON BURR

Burr became vice president after losing the election to Thomas Jefferson. He killed his political rival Alexander Hamilton in a duel and ended his political career in disgrace.

Thomas Jefferson
VP for John Adams

Elbridge Gerry
VP for James Madison

| **Aaron Burr** VP for Thomas Jefferson | **George Clinton** VP for Thomas Jefferson | **George Clinton** VP for James Madison | | |

1801 — 1805 — 1809 — 1812 — 1813 — 1814 — 1817

John Tyler
VP for William Henry Harrison

Millard Fillmore
VP for Zachary Taylor

William R. King
VP for Franklin Pierce

| | **George M. Dallas** VP for James K. Polk | | | **John C. Breckinridge** VP for James Buchanan |

1841 — 1841 (APRIL) — 1845 — 1849 — 1850 — 1853 — 1857 — 1861

Thomas Hendricks
VP for Grover Cleveland

Garret A. Hobart
VP for William McKinley

Theodore Roosevelt
VP for William McKinley

| | **Levi P. Morton** VP for Benjamin Harrison | **Adlai E. Stevenson** VP for Grover Cleveland | | | |

1885 — 1885 (NOVEMBER) — 1889 — 1893 — 1897 — 1899 — 1901 — 1901 (SEPTEMBER)

CHARLES DAWES

Dawes lobbied to limit the use of filibusters (continuous speaking to block the passage of a bill) in the Senate.

Harry S. Truman
VP for Franklin D. Roosevelt

| **Charles Dawes** VP for Calvin Coolidge | **Charles Curtis** VP for Herbert Hoover | **John Nance Garner** VP for Franklin D. Roosevelt | **Henry A. Wallace** VP for Franklin D. Roosevelt |

1925 — 1929 — 1933 — 1941 — 1945

Hubert H. Humphrey
VP for Lyndon B. Johnson

Gerald R. Ford
VP for Richard M. Nixon

Nelson Rockefeller
VP for Gerald R. Ford

WALTER MONDALE

A more powerful vice president than his predecessors, Mondale had weekly luncheons with the president to discuss key issues.

| **Spiro T. Agnew** VP for Richard M. Nixon | | **Walter Mondale** VP for Jimmy Carter | **George H. W. Bush** VP for Ronald Reagan |

1969 — 1973 — 1974 — 1977 — 1981

JOE BIDEN

Biden oversaw measures to revitalize the economy after the 2008 recession, and advised the president on many international issues.

| **Joe Biden** VP for Barack Obama | **Mike Pence** VP for Donald Trump |

2009 — 2017

> Periods of time colored in grey show when the vice presidential office was vacant.

199

POLITICAL PARTIES

The only independent president, George Washington, disliked political parties, but they have since become an integral part of US politics. Since the 1796 elections, there have normally been two main parties, and candidates for the presidency have stood on the platform of one of these.

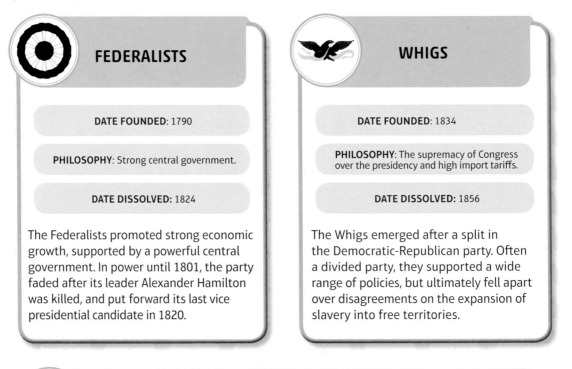

FEDERALISTS

DATE FOUNDED: 1790

PHILOSOPHY: Strong central government.

DATE DISSOLVED: 1824

The Federalists promoted strong economic growth, supported by a powerful central government. In power until 1801, the party faded after its leader Alexander Hamilton was killed, and put forward its last vice presidential candidate in 1820.

WHIGS

DATE FOUNDED: 1834

PHILOSOPHY: The supremacy of Congress over the presidency and high import tariffs.

DATE DISSOLVED: 1856

The Whigs emerged after a split in the Democratic-Republican party. Often a divided party, they supported a wide range of policies, but ultimately fell apart over disagreements on the expansion of slavery into free territories.

DEMOCRATIC-REPUBLICANS

DATE FOUNDED: 1792

PHILOSOPHY: The rights of individual states over the federal government.

DATE DISSOLVED: 1825

The Democratic-Republican party was formed by supporters of Thomas Jefferson, who opposed strong powers for the central government. They aimed to be antielitist and championed the interests of farmers and the working class. The party split in the 1820s, and a faction led by Andrew Jackson became the Democrats.

DEMOCRATS

DATE FOUNDED: 1828 to date

PHILOSOPHY: Strong government, social and economic equality, and government involvement in welfare.

Emerging from the split in the Democratic-Republicans, the Democrats championed the poorer classes. They were dominant until 1860, when they split before the Civil War. This led to a period of Republican dominance until Franklin D. Roosevelt's popular New Deal brought them back to power. The modern Democrat party continues to champion a greater role for government and programs to assist less privileged sections of American society.

REPUBLICANS

DATE FOUNDED: 1854 to date

PHILOSOPHY: Limited government, individual freedom, low taxation.

Founded by antislavery activists, the Republicans had their first president in Abraham Lincoln and the Union's victory in the Civil War gave them 70 years of almost unbroken power. However, the Great Depression brought the Republican dominance to an end. Today's Republican party is more socially conservative with a powerbase in the south and midwest. It continues to support American business interests and to advocate for stronger national defense.

INDEPENDENT CANDIDATES

Although the United States has a two-party system, minor parties and independents have occasionally made their mark. The highest minor party vote was gained by Theodore Roosevelt's Progressive party in 1912, but others, such as the Anti-immigrant "Know Nothing" party in 1856, have also gained a significant percentage of the vote. More recently, independent candidates, such as Ross Perot (right) in 1992, have achieved considerable support due to voter disappointment with the main parties.

Political Parties

PRESIDENTIAL FUN FACTS

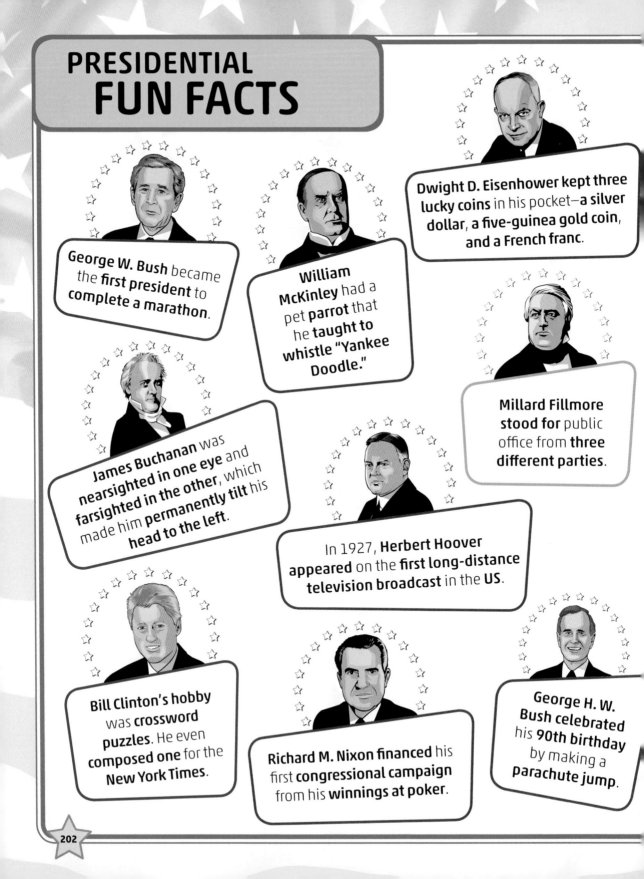

Dwight D. Eisenhower kept three lucky coins in his pocket—a silver dollar, a five-guinea gold coin, and a French franc.

George W. Bush became the first president to complete a marathon.

William McKinley had a pet parrot that he taught to whistle "Yankee Doodle."

Millard Fillmore stood for public office from three different parties.

James Buchanan was nearsighted in one eye and farsighted in the other, which made him permanently tilt his head to the left.

In 1927, Herbert Hoover appeared on the first long-distance television broadcast in the US.

Bill Clinton's hobby was crossword puzzles. He even composed one for the New York Times.

Richard M. Nixon financed his first congressional campaign from his winnings at poker.

George H. W. Bush celebrated his 90th birthday by making a parachute jump.

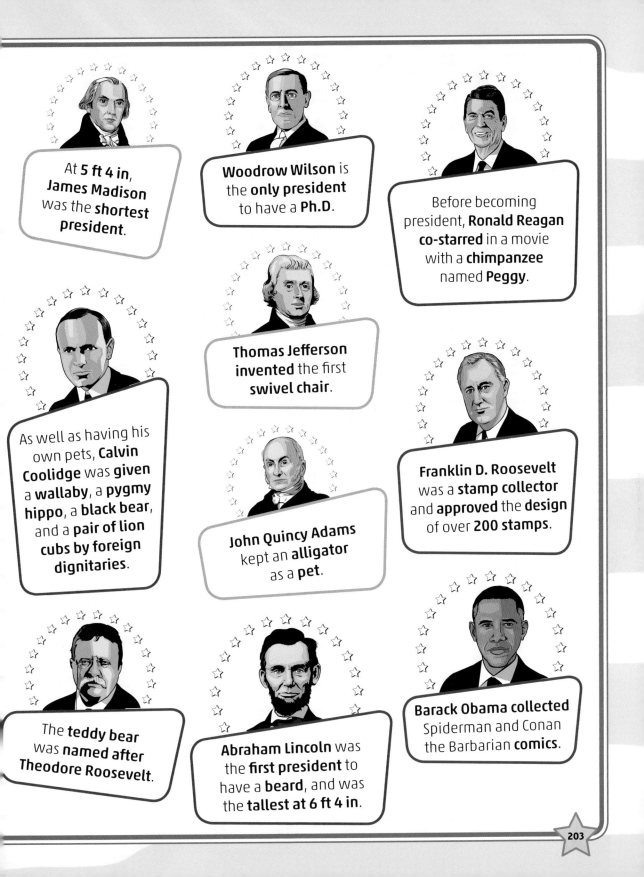

At **5 ft 4 in**, **James Madison** was the **shortest president**.

Woodrow Wilson is the **only president** to have a **Ph.D.**

Before becoming president, **Ronald Reagan co-starred** in a movie with a **chimpanzee** named **Peggy**.

Thomas Jefferson invented the first **swivel chair**.

As well as having his own pets, **Calvin Coolidge** was **given** a **wallaby**, a **pygmy hippo**, a **black bear**, and a **pair of lion cubs** by foreign dignitaries.

John Quincy Adams kept an **alligator** as a **pet**.

Franklin D. Roosevelt was a **stamp collector** and **approved** the **design** of over **200 stamps**.

The **teddy bear** was **named after Theodore Roosevelt**.

Abraham Lincoln was the **first president** to have a **beard**, and was the **tallest at 6 ft 4 in**.

Barack Obama collected Spiderman and Conan the Barbarian **comics**.

GLOSSARY

Abolitionist
A person who called for the abolition of slavery in the United States.

Act
A law that has been passed by Congress and has come into effect.

Amendment
A change to the Constitution of the United States. To come into effect, this must be passed by Congress, and then be ratified by three fourths of all the states.

Anarchist
A person who believes that all forms of central government are unjust and who is often prepared to use any means to overthrow the government.

Budget
The spending plans of a government for a set period of time, showing how much it intends to spend and how much it expects to raise in taxes.

Cabinet
The most senior government officials appointed by the president. They are generally in charge of government departments such as the Treasury.

Capitalism
An economic system where the means of production (such as businesses, factories, and farms) are privately owned with a view to making a profit.

Civil Rights
The right of citizens of a country to equal treatment under the law, regardless of sex, race, or political beliefs.

Civil Service
The people who are employed by the government to run its various departments.

Cold War
The political confrontation between the United States and the Soviet Union (now Russia), in 1947–1991.

Communism
An economic system in which the means of production are owned by the government and wealth is distributed by it.

The Confederacy
The 11 states that broke away from the Union and formed an independent country in 1861. It was dissolved in 1865 at the end of the Civil War.

Congress
The two houses that make up the legislative (law-making) branch of US government. It oversees the national budget and can also impeach the president for misconduct.

Constitutional
When something is allowed by the Constitution. Any acts or measures that are not permitted under the Constitution are referred to as unconstitutional.

Executive
The branch of the US government responsible for implementing and enforcing laws, headed by the president.

Federal
Matters that are under the control of central government, as opposed to individual states.

Founding Fathers
The group of people who played an important role in the foundation of the United States—in particular, those who attended the Constitutional Convention of 1787.

Governor
The head of a state government within the United States.

House of Representatives
One of the two houses of the United States Congress. Members are elected for a two-year term and the number representing each state varies according to the state's population.

Impeachment
The process by which a president or vice president can be removed from office when accused of misconduct. It involves a trial by members of the Senate.

Inauguration
The ceremony at which a newly elected president takes the oath of office and begins his or her presidency.

Inflation
The increase in the level of prices in a country compared to the previous year. When inflation is high, people have to pay far more for the same goods.

Legislation
Measures proposed by the government that are then passed by Congress and become law.

National Debt
The total amount of money owed by a government as a result of spending more than it raises in taxation.

Nationalist
A person who believes that the political and economic interests of their own country are more important than others and who often opposes international cooperation between nations.

Primary (or Caucus)
An election in a state by which delegates are chosen who will then (together with those from other states) select a party's candidate for the presidential election.

Ratification
The process by which an amendment to the Constitution must be accepted by three fourths of all US states before it can come into effect.

Recession
A period when the economy of a country goes into decline.

Reconstruction
The period from 1865–77 during which the states that had formed the Confederacy were placed under military supervision by the federal government, before being admitted back into the Union.

Secession
The act of withdrawing part of a country from the control of the central government, as done by the 11 southern states who left the Union in 1861 and 1862.

Segregation
The practice by which people of different races are forced to use separate schools, workplaces, restaurants, and transportation.

Senate
One of the two houses of the United States Congress. Each state is represented by two senators who are elected for a six-year term.

States' rights
Those rights and powers that are held by individual states as opposed to the federal government.

Suffrage
The right to vote in elections, which was not given to all American men until 1870, and to women until 1920.

Supreme Court
The highest court in the United States. Its nine justices hear appeals from lower courts and decide whether decisions made by them are constitutional or unconstitutional.

Tariff
A tax or duty placed by a government on imports or exports, as a means to control trade or raise money.

Territory
Historically, a region under the control of the federal government, but which is not yet a state.

The Union
The group of states that came together to form the United States, often used to refer to those that did not secede during the Civil War.

Veto
The power of a president to reject any bill that has been passed by Congress.

INDEX

ACKNOWLEDGMENTS

Smithsonian Enterprises:
Kealy Gordon, Product Development Manager
Ellen Nanney, Licensing Manager
Brigid Ferraro, Vice President, Consumer
and Education Products
Carol LeBlanc, Senior Vice President, Consumer
and Education Products
Chris Liedel, President

Curator for the Smithsonian:
James G. Barber, Historian, National Portrait Gallery

Dorling Kindersley would like to thank the following people:
Rupa Rao for editorial assistance and Carron Brown for proofreading and indexing.

Picture Credits
The publisher would like to thank the following for their kind permission to reproduce their photographs:

(Key: a-above; b-below/bottom; c-center; f-far; l-left; r-right; t-top)

2 Dreamstime.com: Timehacker (l). 3 Dreamstime.com: Brandon Seidel. 4 Alamy Stock Photo: IanDagnall Computing (bc); Painting / White House Historical Association (bl). Getty Images: Bettmann (br); Saul Loeb / AFP (cla). 5 Alamy Stock Photo: GL Archive (bl). Getty Images: Brooks Kraft LLC / Corbis (cra). 6 Alamy Stock Photo: Holger Hollemann / dpa (cra). Getty Images: MPI (cla). 6–7 Alamy Stock Photo: Mervyn Rees (b). 7 Alamy Stock Photo: Allstar Picture Library (cla). Getty Images: Raymond Boyd (cra). 8–9 Getty Images: Saul Loeb / AFP. 10–11 Alamy Stock Photo: Tomas Abad. Dreamstime.com: Brett Critchley (All spreads). 12–13 Alamy Stock Photo: Photo Researchers, Inc. 14–15 Courtesy National Gallery of Art, Washington. 15 Library of Congress, Washington, DC: S.W. Fores, 1798 June 1 / LC-DIG-ppmsca-31156 (cr). 16 Alamy Stock Photo: Painting / White House Historical Association. 17 Alamy Stock Photo: Granger Historical Picture Archive. 18–19 The Art Archive: Granger Collection. 20 Getty Images: DeAgostini. 21 Alamy Stock Photo: Archive Images. 22–23 Alamy Stock Photo: Granger Historical Picture Archive. 24–25 Getty Images: GraphicaArtis. 24 Getty Images: Bettmann (bc). 26–27 Mary Evans Picture Library: Everett Collection. 28 Alamy Stock Photo: IanDagnall Computing. 29 Alamy Stock Photo: Granger Historical Picture Archive. 30–31 Getty Images: Universal History Archive. 31 Alamy Stock Photo: Granger Historical Picture Archive (br). 32–33 Alamy Stock Photo: IanDagnall Computing. 33 Alamy Stock Photo: Prisma Archivo (tr). 34 Alamy Stock Photo: IanDagnall Computing. 35 Alamy Stock Photo: Granger Historical Picture Archive. 36–37 Bridgeman Images: Brown, William G. Jr. (19th Century) / © Chicago History Museum, USA. 38–39 Getty Images: Universal History Archive. 39 Getty Images: Bettmann (br). 40 Alamy Stock Photo: IanDagnall Computing. 41 Alamy Stock Photo: Granger Historical Picture Archive. 42–43 Alamy Stock Photo: North Wind Picture Archives. 43 Getty Images: Kean Collection (tr). 44–45 Getty Images: US Library Of Congress. 46 Getty Images: MPI. 47 Getty Images: Fine Art Images / Heritage Images. 48 Alamy Stock Photo: The Art Archive. 49 Alamy Stock Photo: North Wind Picture Archives. 50–51 Getty Images: VCG Wilson / Corbis. 51 Alamy Stock Photo: Everett Collection

Inc (br). 52 Library of Congress, Washington, DC: LC-USZ62-13019. 53 Alamy Stock Photo: North Wind Picture Archives. 54 Library of Congress, Washington, DC: LC-DIG-cwpbh-03741 / Brady-Handy Collection. 55 Getty Images: Bettmann. 56 Library of Congress, Washington, DC: LC-USZ62-13021. 57 Alamy Stock Photo: Granger Historical Picture Archive. 58–59 Getty Images: Ipsumpix / Corbis. 59 Getty Images: Fotosearch (br). 60 Library of Congress, Washington, DC: LC-BH826- 3704. 61 Bridgeman Images: Peter Newark American Pictures. 62 Photoshot: World History Archive. 63 Getty Images: Photo12 / UIG. 64–65 Getty Images: Bettmann. 66 Alamy Stock Photo: Granger Historical Picture Archive. 67 Getty Images: Bettmann. 68–69 Getty Images: Topical Press Agency. 68 Rex by Shutterstock: Everett Collection (bc). 70 Alamy Stock Photo: Archive Pics. 71 Getty Images: US Army Signal Corps / US Army Signal Corps / The LIFE Picture Collection. 72–73 Alamy Stock Photo: Niday Picture Library. 73 Alamy Stock Photo: Granger Historical Picture Archive (br). 74–75 Getty Images: Popperfoto. 74 Getty Images: Fotosearch (bc). 76–77 Alamy Stock Photo: Everett Collection Historical. 77 Alamy Stock Photo: IanDagnall Computing (cr). 78–79 Getty Images: Bettmann. 80 Getty Images: New York Times Co. / Hulton Archive. 81 Getty Images: Bettmann. 82–83 Getty Images: Bettmann. 82 Alamy Stock Photo: Everett Collection Historical (bc). 84–85 Getty Images: Bettmann. 86 Getty Images: Bettmann. 87 Getty Images: Ralph Morse / The LIFE Picture Collection. 88–89 Getty Images: Frank Hurley / NY Daily News Archive. 90 Getty Images: Rolls Press / Popperfoto. 91 Alamy Stock Photo: Pictorial Press Ltd. 92–93 Getty Images: Hulton Archive. 94 Getty Images: Archive Holdings Inc.. 96–97 Getty Images: Arthur Schatz / The LIFE Picture Collection. 98 NASA. 99 Alamy Stock Photo: Granger Historical Picture Archive. 100–101 Getty Images: Bettmann. 101 Bridgeman Images: Pictures from History (br). 102–103 Getty Images: Diana Walker / Time & Life Pictures. 102 Getty Images: Karl Schumacher / AFP (bl). 104–105 Getty Images: Robert R. McElroy. 106 Getty Images: Dirck Halstead / The LIFE Images Collection. 107 Getty Images: Bettmann. 108 Alamy Stock Photo: GL Archive. 109 Getty Images: Pool Chute Du Mur Berlin / Gamma-Rapho. 110–111 Getty Images: Cynthia Johnson / Liaison. 112 Getty Images: Maria Bastone. 113 Alamy Stock Photo: Richard Ellis. 114–115 Getty Images: David McNew. 116 Getty Images: Spencer Platt. 117 Getty Images: Scott Nelson. 118–119 Alamy Stock Photo: White House Photo. 120 Getty Images: Paul J. Richards / AFP. 121 Getty Images: Anthony Behar-Pool. 122 Alamy Stock Photo: UrbanImages (bc). 122–123 Getty Images: Johnny Louis / WireImage. 124–125 Getty Images: Brooks Kraft LLC / Corbis. 126–127 Getty Images: Stock Montage. 128 Alamy Stock Photo: Granger Historical Picture Archive. 129 Alamy Stock Photo: Granger Historical Picture Archive. 130 Alamy Stock Photo: Archive Pics. 131 Alamy Stock Photo: Granger Historical Picture Archive. 132 Getty Images: Bettmann. 133 Getty Images: Bettmann. 134–135 Getty Images: Bettmann. 134 Getty Images: Bettmann (bc). 136 Getty Images: Bettmann. 137 Alamy Stock Photo: CSU Archives / Everett Collection. 138 Rex by Shutterstock: Everett Collection. 139 Getty Images: Bettmann. 140 Getty Images: Diana Walker / Time & Life

Pictures. 141 akg-images. 142 Getty Images: Jeffrey Markowitz / Sygma. 143 Getty Images: Pam Francis / Liaison. 144 Alamy Stock Photo: White House Photo (bc). 144–145 Photoshot: Cheriss May. 146–147 Getty Images: MPI. 148 Getty Images: Ed Vebell. 49 Alamy Stock Photo: Niday Picture Library. 150–151 Getty Images: Bettmann. 152–153 Alamy Stock Photo: Granger Historical Picture Archive. 153 Getty Images: Bettmann (tr). 154 Getty Images: Diana Walker / / Time Life Pictures. 155 Getty Images: Chip Somodevilla. 156–157 Getty Images: Chip Somodevilla. 157 Getty Images: Stephen Jaffe / AFP (br). 158–159 Getty Images: Michael Loccisano. 159 Rex by Shutterstock: Greg Mathieson (br). 160–161 Getty Images: MPI. 161 Getty Images: Universal History Archive (tr). 162–163 akg-images. 162 Alamy Stock Photo: North Wind Picture Archives (bc). 164–165 Alamy Stock Photo: Photo Researchers, Inc. 166–167 Getty Images: Bettmann. 167 akg-images: Imagno (br). 168–169 Getty Images: Stock Montage. 169 Alamy Stock Photo: Archive Pics (br). 170 Getty Images: Keystone-France / Gamma-Keystone. 171 Getty Images: Bettmann. 172–173 Alamy Stock Photo: Holger Hollemann / dpa. 174 123RF.com: Orhan ⬚am (cra). 174–175 Dreamstime.com: Ahdrum. 175 Getty Images: Bettmann (tr). 176–177 Getty Images: Eric Draper / The White House. 178 Getty Images: Bettmann. 179 Getty Images: Raymond Boyd. 180–181 Dreamstime.com: Chrisdoduth. 181 Getty Images: Thomas D. Mcavoy / The LIFE Picture Collection (br). 182 Bridgeman Images: Everett Collection. 183 Getty Images: Bettmann. 184 Getty Images: Smith Collection / Gado (cra); Universal History Archive. 185 123RF.com: Brenda Kean. Alamy Stock Photo: Granger Historical Picture Archive (tr). 186–187 Alamy Stock Photo: Jesse Kraft. 188 Getty Images: Sven Creutzmann / Mambo photo; The LIFE Picture Collection (crb). 189 Getty Images: Alex Wong. 190 Getty Images: Jewel Samad / AFP. 191 Alamy Stock Photo: Allstar Picture Library. 192–193 Getty Images: Raymond Boyd. 196 Alamy Stock Photo: CSU Archives / Everett Collection (crb/Eugene Debs); The Art Archive (fcl). Getty Images: Art Media / Print Collector (tc); Hulton Archive (tr); Encyclopaedia Britannica / UIG (ftr); Kean Collection (cra); Phas / UIG (cl); Hulton Archive (crb); ND / Roger Viollet (cb). Library of Congress, Washington, DC. 196–197 Dreamstime.com: Paul Hakimata. 197 123RF.com: Visions of America LLC (clb). Alamy Stock Photo: GL Archive (cb); GL Archive (cb/Al Gore). Getty Images: Bettmann (tl); Bettmann (ftl); Bettmann (tc/Thomas E. Dewey); Bettmann (tr); Bettmann (ftr). Library of Congress, Washington, DC: Draper, Eric, 1964 / LC-DIG-ppbd-00371 (crb). 198 123RF.com: Mikewaters (bc); Visions of America LLC (br). Getty Images: Library of Congress / Corbis / VCG (cl). 199 Getty Images: Bettmann (tl); Keystone (clb); Library of Congress / Corbis / VCG (cb); Universal History Archive / UIG (bl). 201 Alamy Stock Photo: Luc Novovitch (br).

All other images © Dorling Kindersley

For further information see:
www.dkimages.com